BEFORE YOU GO

General Editors

MATTHEW BENNETT & JOSHUA BOWMAN

BEFORE YOU GO

Wisdom from
10 Men
ON SERVING INTERNATIONALLY

B&H PUBLISHING
BRENTWOOD, TENNESSEE

Copyright © 2024 by Matthew Bennett and Joshua Bowman
All rights reserved.
Printed in the United States of America

978-1-4300-8858-5

Published by B&H Publishing Group
Brentwood, Tennessee

Dewey Decimal Classification: 266
Subject Heading: MISSIONS / EVANGELISTIC WORK / MEN

Unless otherwise noted, all Scripture references are taken from the Christian Standard Bible, copyright © 2017 by Holman Bible Publishers. Used by permission. Christian Standard Bible®, and CSB® are federally registered trademarks of Holman Bible Publishers, all rights reserved.

Scripture references marked ESV are taken from the English Standard Version. ESV® Text Edition: 2016. Copyright © 2001 by Crossway Bibles, a publishing ministry of Good News Publishers.

Scripture references marked NIV are taken from the New International Version, NIV® copyright ©1973, 1978, 1984, 2011 by Biblica, Inc.® Used by permission. All rights reserved worldwide.

Scripture references marked NASB are taken from the New American Standard Bible®, Copyright © 1960, 1971, 1977, 1995, 2020 by The Lockman Foundation. All rights reserved.

Cover design by B&H Publishing Group.
Illustration by ilyakalinin/vectorstock.
Author photos by Scott Huck.

1 2 3 4 5 6 • 27 26 25 24

From Matt:
To Emily—I'm always riding your coattails.

From Josh:
To Wade Coker—my first team leader who showed me the ropes.

Acknowledgments

As this project has come together, we have been consistently blown away by the willingness of the various contributors to share their wisdom, allow us to poke and prod their chapters, and to put together some incredible chapters. We want to kick this book off with an acknowledgment of our gratitude for the men who wrote these chapters and made this book what it is. We believe that their contributions have really made this a valuable resource for folks preparing to head to the mission field. As such, we believe the Lord is going to use their words and wisdom to expand the impact of the gospel all over the globe. Thank you gentlemen.

We also want to make sure to thank our wives whose efforts in the companion volume gave birth to this current volume. Thank you for the idea for this type of book, Emily, and thank you Amy for your contribution to the companion volume. This book exists because you paved the way.

Finally, we wanted to thank B&H for their willingness to publish this two-volume set. To Mary Wiley—you've been a joy to work with and your encouragement of both books has been a consistent source of motivation to keep going. We are so grateful for all those who have had a role in making this book a reality.

May it serve as a resource to prompt reflection, help preparation, and to point you in a faithful direction as you follow the Lord into what he has in the future. To God be the glory in all of our labors.

Contents

Introduction
Matt Bennett 1

Chapter 1: Discerning Your Calling 5
Matt Bennett

Chapter 2: Leaving What You Love 23
Ryan Robertson

Chapter 3: Identity and Task 39
Jeff Kelly

Chapter 4: Integrity and Accountability 53
D. Scott Hildreth

Chapter 5: Serving Well as a Team 71
Josh Bowman

Chapter 6: Prayer and Evangelism 87
Joe Allen III

Chapter 7: Going Single 103
Matt Rhodes

Chapter 8: Family and Mission 117
    Brian Harrell

Chapter 9: Suffering and the Missionary Life 133
    Brooks Buser

Chapter 10: The Spiritual Life of a Missionary 149
    Zane Pratt

Conclusion. 163
    Josh Bowman

Contributors' Biographies 167

Notes. 173

Introduction

Matt Bennett

BROTHER, WE ARE glad that you picked up this book. In fact, we are glad for a couple of reasons. First, if you're reading this book, it is likely that you are somewhere along the path to exploring what God might have for you in missions. Wherever that leads, it is good that you seek the Lord's guidance toward what he would have you do for his glory among the nations. We pray this book will play a part in that discernment and preparatory process.

Second, we are glad you picked up this book because the men who have contributed are some of our dear friends whose wisdom and advice we have admired for a long time. We are glad that you will be able to hear from men who we consider to be some of the cream of the crop. We trust their words will challenge, encourage, and sharpen you.

While many of these guys could write academic tomes of thick theology and robust missiology—and many of them already have done exactly that—the purpose of this book is not to impress or overwhelm you with their intelligence and eloquence. Instead, think of reading each chapter as the chance to sit down over coffee with a guy just a few steps down the road from you. This compilation is like having an opportunity to hear from them, reflect on their experiences, and let their advice help shape the beginning of your missions journey.

As I reflect on my training for missions, I appreciate various elements. The theological preparation in the classroom as I pursued my MDiv was valuable and necessary. I think the training in cross-cultural living provided was also vital to my family's health on the field. The men and women who shared the good, the bad, and the holy parts of their mission experiences stand out as the most formative for my heart and ministry. The stories that they told illustrated the biblical convictions we learned in class and brought theology to life. Their tenacity in the face of adversity gave examples of holy courage that I aspired to emulate. And their advice along the way—advice won by mistakes, struggles, and victories of their own—helped me avoid many pitfalls.

The education and the training I received was important and essential. However, sharing a meal or a conversation with these men and women afforded me the chance to hear storied examples of how training had come to life in practice. While it would undoubtedly be better for you to have that type of face-to-face exposure to these men and their families, we trust that this book will help provide you access to some of the advice they would give even if you never get the opportunity to spend time together.

The men in this volume have served in various missions agencies, in diverse geographic locations, and multiple leadership capacities. We will introduce you to the authors at the start of each chapter, but for now, just know that they represent faithful brothers leading missions strategy, those with experience on the front lines, and those who train and oversee mission teams. These

INTRODUCTION

men are men of character, missiological wisdom, and significant experience in the areas about which they are writing. Each of them brings unique expertise to the topic they are covering along with some lived experience that gives their words credibility.

CHAPTER 1

Discerning Your Calling

Matt Bennett

From the General Editor

MATT BENNETT'S LOVE for the church first became apparent to me as we sat in a doctoral seminar together at Southeastern Seminary in 2015. In this chapter on missionary calling, Matt navigates this topic that, unfortunately, is often riddled with confusion and mystery. I (Josh) believe this chapter will help you grasp clear biblical definitions and offer practical evaluation tools while reminding you of both the missionary task and the role of the local church—the primary agent of God's mission.

As Matt's colleague at Cedarville University, I have seen a steady flow of students in and out of his office seeking counsel as they discern God's call. I have witnessed his faithful service as an elder at his local church as he trains and sends those called to reach the nations. The Lord has used Matt's missionary service, writing, and teaching to reach a broad audience, and I am glad you can learn from him as well as you read this chapter. I appreciate our weekly lunches at the cafeteria with this godly man, dear friend, and like-minded missiologist.

As you seek to discern or confirm your part in the Great Commission (Matt. 28:19–20), I trust you will have a clearer understanding of God's call. I trust this will be a valuable resource to pastors and leaders as you take your role as a sender seriously. And before many of you go, I pray your confidence will not be in an individual, isolated self-affirmation but the corporate blessing of a spirit-filled congregation.

I'M CALLED—NOW WHAT?

As a young man, I remember walking out of the exhibit hall at the missions conference with more fliers, brochures, and ballpoint pens than I could hold. My mind was swirling with questions. But, at the same time, I was exhilarated by the prospect of unknown adventures with God. I had come to this conference with a bit of hesitation regarding my future. But I would be leaving with a confidence that I would not have believed possible: God was calling me—and my future wife, Emily—to missions. The only questions remaining were the details of where, when, and with which agency.

Once we had returned home, the hype faded a bit as we surveyed the brochures strewn across my desk. All the agencies we had talked with emphasized the urgent needs their missionaries were meeting. Most promised to equip and deploy us to join God on the frontiers of lostness amidst pressing human suffering. The problem was that they all spoke of different countries, continents, and contexts. My excitement quickly turned to anxiety as I had to say yes to one—which consequently meant saying no to the others. What if I chose wrong?

WHAT DOES CALLING MEAN?

Can you relate to the story above? Have you ever attended a conference like this or a missions event that moved your heart? Did you also feel paralyzed by all the options? I regularly find myself counseling university students in this type of scenario. While a calling to missions often involves a stirring of the heart with a burden for the nations in general, it also requires deliberation and decisions about specific details.

Before we try to untie the knot of the details and decisions about your calling, though, it is important to make sure we are clear on what the word *calling* means. In Christian circles, calling has come to mean a variety of things. Some use calling to describe a vague feeling they got after reading a missionary biography like *To the Golden Shore*. Others may point to moments in their life where they confidently believe that God concretely and irreversibly told them they would be missionaries.

Despite the breadth of common usage, our primary concern should be to ask, "How does the Bible use 'calling' language?" We need to address this foundational issue before assuming our definitions have biblical warrant. Clarifying this biblical understanding of calling will lead to clarification in the details. And, while clarity around the idea of calling is important as you launch, it will also provide ballast on the hard days ahead. In fact, I am arguing that clarity in your calling will help you walk as one who is in Christ, under the commission of the Word, and according to the communal affirmation of your calling by the church.

CALLED IN CHRIST

The New Testament mainly uses the language of calling in reference to our relationship with God in Christ. There are few more precious words applied to humans than the oft-repeated pair: *in Christ*. Paul talks about being "in Christ" over and over throughout his letters and connects this positional reality with all sorts of privileges, responsibilities, and blessings.

Consider Paul's exalted language connecting our calling to be "in Christ" throughout Ephesians. For instance, Ephesians 1:3–4 (emphasis mine) begins the letter by saying:

> Blessed is the God and Father of our Lord Jesus Christ, who has blessed us with every spiritual blessing in the heavens *in Christ*. For he *chose us in him*, before the foundation of the world, to be holy and blameless in love before him.

The two places that I have italicized above reinforce the connection between our calling and our position in Christ—we have been blessed and chosen in Christ. The letter goes on in verses 18–19 to articulate Paul's prayer for the church:

> I pray that the eyes of your heart may be enlightened so that you may know what is the hope of his calling, what is the wealth of his glorious inheritance in the saints, and what is the

immeasurable greatness of his power toward us who believe, according to the mighty working of his strength.

Here, Paul's continued line of thought connects our calling to hope in Christ with the fact that we have been chosen in and united to him. And again, in Ephesians 4:1–6, Paul makes this holy calling in Christ explicit as he urges the Ephesians along, writing:

> Therefore I, the prisoner in the Lord, urge you to walk worthy of the calling you have received, with all humility and gentleness, with patience, bearing with one another in love, making every effort to keep the unity of the Spirit through the bond of peace. There is one body and one Spirit—just as you were called to one hope at your calling—one Lord, one faith, one baptism, one God and Father of all, who is above all and through all and in all.

Note how, throughout the letter, Paul connects our salvation with our calling. Such a calling and salvation is accomplished for and extended to those who have believed in Christ Jesus. And those who believe in Christ are called into his corporate body—a body manifested in local expressions of church.

To be biblically grounded in our understanding of "calling" language, we must start by recognizing the common calling that precedes and shapes any particular callings discerned by a believer. Before speaking about "our calling" in its unique contours or vocational details, we must realize that its particulars must emerge from this universal call. Called to be in Christ, every disciple is then caught up into Christ's mission. That means that each disciple called to be in Christ is called to be a disciple-maker, as the next section will demonstrate. Such a calling comes to us not mystically, but as we work through the pages of the Bible. The second aspect of discerning our calling, then, must be to consider how God's Word features in our discernment process.

CALLED BY THE WORD TO MAKE DISCIPLES OF ALL NATIONS

You have probably heard the well-worn pastoral quip that goes: "If you want to hear God speak, read the Bible. If you want to hear God speak audibly, read the Bible out loud." While there is a sense in which this adage is a cheeky pastoral reminder of what we have in God's Word, the truth of the matter is more profound than cheeky.

While the Lord uses the events of our lives to get our attention or attune us to certain things we are otherwise prone to miss, the events of our lives are not self-interpreting. Nor do they explain the beautiful mystery of our calling in Christ. Therefore, we begin looking for our calling in Christ and the myriad implications of that calling by consulting Scripture. At the end of his earthly ministry, Jesus called his disciples to a task that stretches across the ages and extends to present-day disciples in what many refer to as the Great Commission.

In the Great Commission, the task given to the church is a command from the One to whom all authority in heaven and on earth has been given (Matt. 28:18). It is a task that is undertaken by the empowering of his presence with his people. It is not some optional add-on, but something at the very core of a disciple's identity and purpose.

The Great Commission calls all disciples to be involved in making disciples, teaching them to obey all that Jesus commanded, and receiving new believers into the community by practicing baptism in the name of the triune God (vv. 19–20). More than merely a missionary text, the Great Commission calls all disciples to be disciple-makers irrespective of where they find themselves.

However, the part that becomes uniquely relevant for considering the calling to missions is that phrase that follows the command, "make disciples *of all nations*" (v. 19a, emphasis mine). While many disciples will make disciples in the places and among the people who are their immediate neighbors, friends, and family, some nations are outside the reach of disciples and churches. If all nations are the target of our global mission, then some will not only be *called* to be disciple-makers, they will also be *sent* to be disciple-makers.

As I noted above, I often counsel students who are discerning their calling to the mission field. After asking them about their testimony and church involvement, I ask, "Who are you discipling today? Where are you sharing the gospel today?" You will not establish these skills and habits simply by getting on a plane. And, from the perspective of your church, do you really think they should send you somewhere else to do what you are not doing at home? In fact, the final stage of discerning the details of your calling is to recognize that the local church is integral to affirming your aspiration.

BEFORE YOU GO

CALLED BY THE CHURCH

This is perhaps where things get most interesting for determining the calling to missions. Previous generations of Christians have been raised in churches where one's spiritual gifts—and often the subsequent service they pursue in the church—are determined by the results of a quiz taken individually online or in a magazine tear-out somewhere. As it pertains to missions, often someone individually becomes interested in and passionate about missions due to some conference or exposure to the plight of the lost. So they begin to refer to themselves as being called to missions. The common factor in these approaches to discernment is that it often remains an individual assessment.

At the beginning of this chapter, I told my own story of trying to discern my call by myself. I had been exposed to the need for missionaries to take the gospel to those lacking access. I had offered the Lord my willingness to say yes to whatever he would ask of me. And I had surrendered my vision of what I wanted my life to look like. I walked out of that exhibit hall sure that I could say, "I am called to missions."

But if we look at what Paul said in 1 Corinthians, my calling in Christ also calls me into a body of believers. I am not called to be a hand or a leg independent of a body (12:12–27). Therefore, it is probably too soon to say, "I am called," if no one else has yet affirmed that calling.[1] To put it starkly, those aspiring to the role of a missionary should not refer to themselves as *called* to missions until their church has *sent* them. Prior to being sent, it is probably better to simply say something like the following: "I think that the Lord is burdening my heart for the nations. In order to discern what the Holy Spirit might be doing in my life, I am seeking the counsel and affirmation of my church."

This is not just a preferred way to approach missions, though. It has a precedent in Scripture. In Acts 13:1–5, we see Barnabas and Saul gathered with the saints in the church at Antioch when the Spirit confirmed that he was setting them apart for a specific task. The church affirmed this, laid hands on them, and sent them out as the first missionary team commissioned by the church in the New Testament. Not only does the church have a role in the discernment of this calling, but they also help to maintain accountability to that calling. When they returned after their first missionary journey, Barnabas and Saul gathered the church elders in Antioch to gave an account of the work they had been faithful to fulfill (14:26–28).

The church helped discern the calling, affirmed it through sending, and kept Barnabas and Saul accountable. Of course, as with much of the material in Acts, this is a descriptive account. It does not contain a set of imperative instructions that would be definitively binding upon the contemporary church. But still, this is the example that we have, and it is an example that fits with the vision of the church given throughout the rest of the Bible. I believe we are on good ground to derive our sense of calling to a specific task from our church's affirmation and sending to that task. Still, you might be asking some practical questions about how to invite the church into that discernment process. Let me offer a few practical examples of ways you can invite your church into the discernment process.

BEFORE YOU GO

A DECISION-MAKING VENN DIAGRAM

I am convinced that a good old Venn diagram will help solve most of the problems in life. This may be an overstatement, but you remember these from grade school, no doubt. A Venn diagram has two or more overlapping circles with a focal point created at the intersection in the center.

As I counsel students who ask what they should do with their lives, I often draw a Venn diagram and label the circles as follows: Passions & Desires, Skills & Abilities, Needs & Opportunities. It is worth explaining each of these categories for clarity. So, let's begin by unpacking what might fall into the category of each of these circles of our example. The goal is to see where the three overlap, helping the students begin to discern how the Lord might lead them.

Passions & Desires

God has made each of us unique. This means that some of us love the outdoors and adventure, while others love staying inside in a climate-controlled environment. Some of us love music, while others prefer sports. The list could go on and on. Sometimes, however, in determining our calling, we can fall into one of two ditches as we assess the role passions and desires play in discerning our calling.

One of the ditches we can fall into is to be of the persuasion that God wants us to be happy doing *only* what we love to do. Thus, we assume he would only call us to tasks involving the things we love. Sacrificing our preferences is not on our radar. This can be detrimental for those asked to take on the discomfort of traveling to a new country, learning a new language, eating new foods, and observing new cultural norms. Nevertheless, there are certain aspects of our preferences that we will have to lay down if we are to follow Jesus. After all, Jesus said that following him would require taking up our cross (Matt. 16:24).

The other ditch we can fall into, though, is assuming that *everything* we like to do must be put to death if we are to follow him. Believing that following Jesus should feel like a sacrifice in every way, we assume that our natural inclinations must be leading us away from God's will for our lives. This can be dangerous because it assumes that God did not, in some respect, give us these passions and desires to be used for his glory. It can cause us to assume that God's will cannot cohere with how he has shaped us and fashioned our passions and desires.

Instead of falling into either of those ditches, I think it is wise to consider what tasks and activities bring you joy and can be leveraged to God's glory. Is there something about the unique passions and desires the Lord has given you that can help determine where you might consider going as a missionary? Is there something about your passions and desires that helps to make you a fit for a specific missionary task and approach? These questions, asked in concert with people in your church, can help you start to discern how the Lord has shaped you for ministry. Then, once you have determined some of your passions and desires, it is good to think through how those passions and desires translate into skills and abilities.

Skills & Abilities

In addition to your passions, it is necessary to consider what skills and abilities you have. I usually tell my students that sometimes there is a distinct difference between what they like and what they can do. For example, I like music and singing in the shower. But due to my complete lack of skill and gifting musically, it is obvious that it is not a part of my calling to use music as a means of ministry.

In this sphere, the goal is to reflect on and ask others to speak into areas of your life that they would identify as specific areas of natural talent, acquired skill, or even formal credentials. These skills and abilities may open doors for you to participate in a particular task or vocation. Basically, this circle inspects things that you can do well that can contribute to clarifying your calling to a specific type of ministry.

For example, if you have a passion for exploring culture and worldview and have acquired a degree in linguistics, these factors will play into your decisions. It may be that Bible translation is the type of work that you and your church decide that you should explore. On the other hand, if you grew up on a farm and have a green thumb, you may find that the Lord is calling you to explore agricultural inroads into isolated, rural communities for gospel proclamation, disciple-making, and church-planting.

While you can reflect on each of these issues for yourself, I think having your church weigh in on this assessment is essential. There are certain things that we know better about ourselves than anyone else does. At the same time, those observing us in the covenant community of the church can also provide insights that we may not have identified in ourselves. In addition to that, the church can be an important help in narrowing the field of possible missions assignments.

Needs & Opportunities

This brings us to the final circle. Where are the strategic needs for missions work that align with our passions and abilities? Where might we plug into the ongoing work that our church is doing? Where might our church be strategically looking to start a new work? These questions, asked in concert with your local church, can help narrow your options sufficiently enough to help you avoid that sense of paralysis from knowing there are needs everywhere.

As you and your church discern your shape and fit for missions, it is helpful to begin by asking whether or not any of your church's existing missionary partners might have a specific need for someone with your skill set. Likewise, your church may know of expressed needs in other fields that match your gifts and passions. Or, as was the case for my wife and me, your church may already be gathering a team to engage a new field of ministry where your skills and gifts would serve well.

When you and your church find that these three circles overlap—that your gifts, your passions, and the strategic opportunities are made known—I think you are justified in taking steps forward in that direction. Just be sure to do so prayerfully, asking the Lord to keep the door shut if this is not where he is leading.

THE CHURCH SENDS THE CALLED

At the beginning of the chapter, I led with the story of my wife and me standing over a desk strewn with brochures for various agencies and a dizzying sense of uncertainty about how to proceed. However, one thing that became clear to us was that missions seemed to be defined differently for each agency. Some saw the task as mere evangelization, while others prioritized humanitarian efforts—hoping that one might name Jesus as the reason for our compassion.

As we reflected on Scripture and the Great Commission, we realized that what we wanted to be a part of was the strategic work of bringing the gospel and its implications to bear on places and people lacking access. This would likely require crossing geographic, language, and cultural barriers and boundaries. Once having crossed those barriers and boundaries, though, we saw the Great Commission as requiring us to engage in more than mere evangelism, but fully-orbed disciple-making and church-planting.

And in the end, we wanted to not only make disciples, but to train disciple-makers. We didn't want only to plant churches, but to plant churches that would plant other churches and send their own missionaries.

Our church's leadership realized that we would need further preparation to do that. We figured that if we wanted to be medical doctors in another country, we would need to know what medicine we were injecting into our patients' veins. How much more so, we reasoned, would we need to be adept in diagnosing and applying the gospel and doctrine to the souls of those among whom we would minister? After all, if we were in a pioneer missions setting, what we taught and modeled would set the trajectory for the church in that place. So, we found a seminary that would allow us to prepare and engage in missions.

We went to seminary with a vague attraction to the continent of Africa and with our home church's blessing to pursue this direction for our lives. Upon enrolling, we discovered that our cohort was designed to focus on Muslim communities. In addition, we joined a church that had a passion and dedication for missions. Within a year of joining, our church began a missionary training pipeline and announced that they were starting to pray that God would raise a team to go to one of two Muslim-majority nations in North Africa. So we joined the cohort, and the Lord connected our hearts and lives with three other people. As we progressed through the training pipeline, our church continued to affirm our fit for this ministry.

It was seven years between that day that we stood over the pile of brochures and the moment our feet first hit the ground in North Africa. But all along the way, the Lord used his church to affirm aspects of our ministry, shape and direct our preparation, lay hands on us, and affirm our aspiration to the mission field as a calling.

There is much more I could tell you about our time and our church's role in our lives. But when we had hard days, it was helpful to look back to that commissioning and recognize that we had been sent by brothers and sisters and not merely by our own whims. Likewise, when we had joyous days, it was an incredible privilege to share the fruit the Lord allowed us to see with our church. And even as we transitioned off the field, it was our church that affirmed for us that it was the right path.

Brother, I would plead with you to engage your church in this process. Don't let your idea of calling be something that is just between you and the Lord. Lean into the brothers and sisters in Christ who are part of your church to evaluate, commission, and support you as a corporate affirmation of your calling.

DISCUSS AND REFLECT

1. As you consider your role in missions, where do the Bible, your internal desires, your external circumstances, and the church's affirmation all align? Where might they not align?

2. What counsel does your local church give you as you prayerfully consider where and how to serve? How have you sought to be known and evaluated in your sense of calling by the church?

3. What character traits should you seek to develop as you prepare to serve as a missionary? How can you begin demonstrating the skills of a disciple-maker now?

4. Who in your sending community will be willing to remind you of the church's affirmation of your calling on difficult days? Who can you reach out to in order to let your church celebrate the work the Lord is doing through you?

CHAPTER 2

Leaving What You Love

Ryan Robertson

From the General Editor

OVER THE PAST few years I (Matt) have gotten to know Ryan Robertson through his role as the president of Reaching & Teaching International Ministries (RTIM). The Lord has given Ryan an important voice in contemporary missiology and is using him to lead a growing agency committed to healthy, church-centered missions. As our paths have crossed and friendship has developed, I have found Ryan to be a man who has a keen mind, deep convictions, and an insatiable desire to see the knowledge of God cover the earth as water covers the sea (Hab. 2:14).

Being a Canadian who is living outside of his home country and removed from family, Ryan personally understands some of what it takes to uproot life and relocate to a place and task that requires leaving. Likewise, in his role leading RTIM, Ryan regularly counsels those who are preparing to leave what they love in order to follow King Jesus. This makes him the perfect candidate to write this chapter.

As you read Ryan's story, his exposition, and his advice, I pray that you will be encouraged to see more than what you are leaving behind. I pray that before you go, you also begin to count the joy of following Jesus where he leads. Would it be that your preparation to leave would be characterized by a confident joy that you are following the One who asks everything of us yet who provides even more.

HOME IN THE REARVIEW

It was just after Christmas. My wife, Erin, and I were sitting in front of her parents at a restaurant in Toronto, Canada. I was three months into a six-month treatment for Hodgkin's lymphoma, on a tough biweekly regiment of chemotherapy. My oncologist had just given me approval to move to the United States with my family to take a job with Reaching & Teaching International Ministries and pursue a doctoral degree at The Southern Baptist Theological Seminary in Louisville, Kentucky. What we weren't prepared for was the news that my father-in-law was beginning tests for a terminal neurological condition that would ultimately end his life thirty months later.

For the next six months we wrestled through the last birthdays and holidays at home. Our family and local church had been such integral parts of our everyday lives. We were within a sixty-minute drive of all of our immediate family members. I was on staff at our church and the elders, staff, and members had been incredibly supportive to me throughout my diagnosis and treatment. We had benefited greatly from a health-care system in which I was healed of lymphoma with no medical bills. We lived in a wonderful neighborhood three minutes from the Christian school where our kids attended and Erin taught. We loved their classmates and teachers.

Once a week, I would get a phone call or text from my dad inviting me to grab lunch. We'd eat at one of the fast-food restaurants close to my office and catch up on family, life, and sports. I specifically remember getting into my car after our last lunch before we moved and crying my way back to the office, feeling the impending loss of our weekly ritual.

Our family of five really struggled through leaving so many things that we loved. Our church. Our family. Our friends. Our home. Our neighborhood. The Lord had been incredibly kind to us; we loved so many parts of our life in Canada. As much as we looked forward to what the Lord had in store for us, our last six months at home were filled with the hardness of giving up those good things and trying our best to teach our kids to trust the Lord in what lay ahead.

As we headed south, my heart was heavy knowing that, for the next season, Canada would grow smaller in the rearview mirror as we transitioned into our new life in a new land.

This transition was emotional, formative, and monumental for our family. In my time in the Word during that season I took comfort in the fact that there are many in Scripture who left home to follow God's lead. And though I won't try to baptize our situation with biblical metaphor and parallel—pretending that this was our exodus or our exile—that does not mean the Bible is silent on our situation. I took great solace in Jesus's words regarding those who would leave home behind to follow him.

BEFORE YOU GO

MARK 10:29–30

"Truly I tell you," Jesus said, "there is no one who has left house or brothers or sisters or mother or father or children or fields for my sake and for the sake of the gospel, who will not receive a hundred times more, now at this time—houses, brothers and sisters, mothers and children, and fields, with persecutions—and eternal life in the age to come."

I remember reading these verses soon after our move. A number of things stood out to me in Jesus's words and continue to encourage me on the hard days. First, Jesus acknowledges that something is being left behind. Second, Jesus affirms that there is a purpose for leaving. Third, Jesus establishes the promise of what is to come.

In the broader context of this passage, Jesus had just had a conversation with a rich young man who asked him what he must do to inherit eternal life. Jesus responded by telling the young man that he must leave all he had, give away his wealth, and follow him (vv. 17–22). While this interaction with the rich young man was personal, the words we just read from Jesus are more broadly applicable to readers from that time on through our own. The principle and the invitation land on us as much as they did on him.

Of course, we are not all called to leave the same things but we are all called to love Jesus most and follow him. For some Christians, that means being obedient to Jesus without moving somewhere for the sake of ministry. It means selflessly pouring oneself out to serve the church and community in a place that is and has always been home. For others, it means leaving what you love. For all of us, it means finding our greatest satisfaction in Jesus and laying down anything that he asks.

In contrast to some of the messages that are broadcast about following Jesus today, it is worth reading through the Bible to ask what it costs people to follow Jesus. What you will find is that Jesus never downplays the fact that there will be a cost.

In Mark 10:29–30, Jesus lists three specific things that might be left behind to follow him: house, family, and fields. I don't think this list is exhaustive, but it is representative. Furthermore, I am not sure what that cost will be for you or which aspect of leaving will seem most costly.

It might be that the act of "leaving house" will be the most profound. Your home may be a place of stability, a place of belonging, a place where you are known by others. For many of us, our homes are our place of comfort and retreat. It may be the place you grew up and the place where you've made the most memories.

Or perhaps it is not your physical place that is so important to you, but the fact that you are leaving your people hits hard. Leaving siblings, parents, or even your own children to follow Jesus might be the weightiest part of your departure. We were very close to our family in Canada. We ate many meals together, our parents attended all of the events at our kids' school, and we had readily available (and free) childcare whenever we wanted a date night. Included among our people that we had to leave were our brothers and sisters in Christ who were members of our local church. We had raised and discipled our kids alongside some of them, had walked through difficult things together, and held each other accountable.

The third category of things left behind that Jesus includes is our "fields." I read this as leaving behind my livelihood. As a husband and dad, I have a responsibility to provide for my family, and to an extent, by leaving Canada I was sacrificing a sure thing—a job I had held for seven years with a steady income. In exchange, I was planning to take on a role in a foreign country that required me to raise financial support. I had to solicit funds from the very family, friends, and local church that I was leaving.

All three categories of "things left" that Jesus mentions in Mark 10 touched on categories in which I found comfort and that made it hard to leave. My home, my people, and my work.

But I told you earlier that there were three things that stood out to me in this passage. Second, and beyond what was left behind, I found myself drawn to consider Jesus's words regarding the reason for leaving.

The categories of things left are not unique things to Christians. After all, people leave their homes, people, and employment for a number of reasons that have nothing to do with following Christ. It could be to pursue a job, further education, or adventure on the other side of the planet. However, as Christians, Jesus reminds us that we are leaving these things for his sake and for the sake of the gospel.

Our motivation is not merely a job, education, or adventure. It is Jesus. It is our fundamental belief that he is the Son of God who came to earth, lived a perfect life, died a death he didn't deserve as a willing sacrifice for our sins, and rose from the dead three days later in victory over the grave. It is this gospel call that holds out to us the hope that, "If you confess with your mouth, 'Jesus is Lord,' and believe in your heart that God raised him from the dead, you will be saved" (Rom. 10:9). This is the message that must be proclaimed to billions of lost people around the world and is the motivation behind a Christian's call to leave what they love.

The third thing that stood out to me in Jesus's words in these verses in Mark is the promise of what is to come. Friend, whatever you are being called to leave, know that the eternal reward waiting for you will satisfy you completely in comparison to all you are being called to leave. Yes, it will be hard. Yes, you will have persecutions. There will be people who will revile you because of the gospel to which you hold. But those persecutions and the hardships you face in leaving what you love will pale in comparison to the "absolutely incomparable eternal weight of glory" that awaits us in the new heavens and new earth (2 Cor. 4:17).

With all of this in mind, I want to encourage you with a few of the things that have helped me in the process of grieving loss and fighting for a future-oriented perspective. In my role leading a missionary-sending organization, I find myself giving the following advice to our missionary candidates on a regular basis. I pray that it is encouraging to your heart as you let go of what is behind and grasp what is ahead for King Jesus's sake.

ACKNOWLEDGE THE DIFFICULTY OF LEAVING

In the midst of all of the tasks that need to be completed prior to leaving, I always recommend making a list of all of the people you need to spend some time with and make a plan to spend some meaningful time with them. Make sure you have the opportunity to say everything that needs to be said and don't fall into the temptation of trying to cram your goodbyes into a small window of time. Each goodbye doesn't need to be long, but in your final months at home, endeavor to spend meaningful time with the people you love.

And brother, just know that it is okay to cry when you say goodbye! Maybe expressing emotions is not difficult for you, but I often find that men are reticent to do so for a variety of reasons. For one thing, I think there is a concern that expressing sadness with our loved ones will only compound the feeling. You can love the people you leave well by acknowledging and expressing the difficulty of leaving. Let your friends and family know that they are a gift from the Lord and are evidences of his grace in your life. Words—and yes, even tears—can be powerful ways of demonstrating the importance of a person that you are parting ways with.

REMEMBER GOD'S FAITHFULNESS TO YOU

In the middle of grieving what you are leaving, I would also encourage you to remember the source of those good gifts. Remember that everything that you love and are leaving was ultimately given to you by the Lord. Your family. Your church. Your friends. Your home. Your job. All of those things are good gifts from a good God. He was faithful to save you and has been faithful to sustain you.

Remember that God was faithful to give you the desire to go. I have yet to meet a Christian who didn't desire to follow Jesus at the moment of their salvation. I have yet to meet a missionary who didn't have a desire to "go." Our good desires are given to us by

God by his grace. Remember that. As you're preparing to go, write down those desires. What are you desiring to do and why do you desire to do it? What gifts have been affirmed in you by your local church? What is it about the opportunity that lies ahead of you that fits so well with your desires and gifting? There will be difficult days ahead where you'll be tempted to pack it up and move back because it's too hard and you miss what you love so much. It is important to recall those desires in times of discouragement.

Remember that God has graciously promised to sanctify you. Even in the midst of your weakness, God is at work to conform you into the likeness of his Son (Rom. 8:29), the same Son "Who, being in very nature God, did not consider equality with God something to be used to his own advantage; rather, he made himself nothing by taking the very nature of a servant, being made in human likeness. And being found in appearance as a man, he humbled himself by becoming obedient to death—even death on a cross!" (Phil. 2:6–8 NIV).

Friend, you are an ambassador of the King of kings. What a privilege! He has saved you and you have the privilege of making his gospel known. He has promised to sustain you. He has promised to sanctify you. He has been faithful and he will continue to be faithful. He will never fail you (Deut. 31:6).

BE WATCHFUL FOR IDOLATRY

Often, we take the good gifts that the Lord has given us and turn them into idols. To be honest, the process of leaving what we loved in Canada revealed a number of idols in my heart.

I would encourage you to prayerfully list the things are hard to leave and ask yourself why it's so hard to leave those things behind. Pray the words of David in Psalm 139:23–24: "Search me, God, and know my heart; test me and know my concerns. See if there is any offensive way in me; lead me in the everlasting way."

I know that I struggled with the idols of comfort and belonging to a people and a place. There was the idol of the closeness of our extended family, relationally and geographically. There was the idol of security. I had a stable job at our church, our friendships were stable, and we had access to free health care—which meant a lot, given my cancer was now in remission. I wish I could say that these idols don't creep into my life anymore, but I still struggle with them. I am thankful that my experience of leaving what I loved revealed them and I'm better prepared to identify them when my heart wanders.

CARE WELL FOR THE ONES YOU ARE LEAVING WITH

In leaving to go, make sure to be realistic with your expectations for yourself and those for whom you are responsible. You will have hard days ahead. I remember early conversations with our tearful children as they mourned what they'd left behind and questioned why we made them do so. In my hardest days, I worried that our kids would grow up to hate me for moving them away from all that they loved in their life. The way that I fought this worry was to try to keep everyone upbeat and to put on a brave face, even when I was personally missing "home."

I found that I was often tempted toward three things. First, I was tempted to avoid the conversation altogether. Second, I was tempted to simply refocus their attention on all the "good things" that the Lord had given us in our new home: there were new friendships, they now were being homeschooled by their mom with a new flexibility on when we took vacations, and they loved our new local church. Finally, I was tempted to become frustrated with them for not being cheerful about our new life. Thankfully, my wife has a different constitution than me. She was able to gently remind me that we made this decision, our kids did not.

Be appropriately vulnerable with your family. Don't share things that would be unhelpful, but acknowledging that leaving is hard for you will help your kids deal with their own emotions in leaving. If you're married, have regular conversations with your spouse to check in on each other. Be willing to shed some more tears together and be quick to encourage each other with how the Lord is encouraging you in your new home. Look for ways to encourage your family with the gospel. Fight the temptation to avoid the conversation altogether.

LOOK FORWARD TO WHAT THE LORD HAS IN STORE FOR YOU

Finally, as you are following the Lord toward this next stage of life and ministry, don't forget to look even beyond this next season to the ultimate horizon. Like a marathon runner, don't simply fix your eyes on the next water station, but consider the finish line that is yet to come.

In fact, I can relate to this imagery of a runner in search of a finish line. I ran a marathon at Disney World in 2011. The first half was fun. My body didn't hurt too much in the beginning. Adrenaline was coursing through my body and the excitement of running alongside thousands of others carried me forward. That all changed at the 18-mile mark. My IT bands started to ache. Then the pain became excruciating. It hurt more to walk than run, and so I just put one foot in front of the other for the last 8.2 miles. I questioned my sanity. *Why would I volunteer to run a marathon in the first place? Who does that? Would my legs ever feel the same?* Around the 21-mile mark, a group of us had to come to a sudden stop when a spectator walked in front of us, and it took every ounce of my will to start running again. What kept me moving when every cell in my body was screaming to give up? It was the anticipation of the joy I would have when I crossed the finish line and hugged Erin and our little ones. It was knowing that they would be cheering me on in that moment.

In 1 Corinthians 9:24, Paul reminds us that the Christian life is like a race and should be "run in such a way to win the prize." The writer of Hebrews encourages us to "run with endurance" (12:1). The Christian life is a marathon and there are inevitable hardships along the way. There may be times in your ministry that every cell in your body is imploring you to give up. It's in these moments that you must fix your eyes on the prize. There is a great and unimaginable prize awaiting you at the finish line. Put one foot in front of the other and anticipate what is ahead when you cross that finish line and fall into the arms of your Savior. In Mark 10:30, Jesus promises a reward that surpasses what we could even imagine. Receiving a reward that is infinitely greater than what has been left seems incomprehensible. But it is reality. When you are tempted to look back at what you are leaving, choose to look forward to what the Lord has in store for you.

LEAVING AND ARRIVING

Looking back on our family's experience of leaving Canada, I wish I could say that everything went smoothly from day one in our new home. But it didn't. Our kids had tough nights where they tearfully asked us why we had to leave their friends and their family. We had humbling visits back to Canada where we realized that our families, friends, local church, and colleagues had all moved on without us. It was specifically difficult when we returned home for a couple of months at the beginning of the Covid-19 pandemic. Our kids' Baba, my father-in-law, passed away and we grieved not only the end of his life but also the years we missed being with him.

As time went on, the tough nights became fewer. There are still hard days, and they come without warning. Sometimes it's a life event of a family member that is missed, like a wedding. At other times, it's triggered by small and trivial things. I remember a weird sadness when our hometown Toronto Raptors won the NBA Finals. While our former neighborhood was doubtless caught up in the celebration of the hometown victory, I was saddened by the small fact that our kids wouldn't be able to attend the parade. I expect that we'll always feel a tinge of sadness when we think of what we've left.

Yet at this point, several years removed from the initial move, we have grown to love our new home, our new people, and our new roles. Our kids made new friends and are loving learning in their new school. We have folded into our new local church and I've never enjoyed work as much as I do now. I'm most thankful for all that I learned about God's faithfulness and my own heart in leaving what I loved. Should the Lord call us to do something new one day or lead our family to remain in our current assignment, we have learned what it means to find our ultimate satisfaction in him. Because wherever he calls us to live out our mortal days, we know that our true reward awaits us when we are raised immortal.

It's oddly comforting to know that we aren't the only ones who have ever left what we love for the sake of Christ. I have been particularly encouraged by this recollection of John Paton, the well-known missionary to the New Hebrides. He described the six-mile walk he took with his dad as he departed his family home:

> For the last half-mile or so we walked on together in almost unbroken silence, my father, as often was his custom, carrying hat in hand, while his long, flowing yellow hair (then yellow, but in later years white as snow) streamed like a girl's down his shoulders. His lips kept moving in silent prayers for me; and his tears fell fast when our eyes met each other in looks for which all speech was vain. We halted on reaching the appointed parting place; he grasped my hand firmly for a minute in silence, and then, solemnly and affectionately said, "God bless you, my son! Your father's God prosper you, and keep you from all evil."
>
> Unable to say more, his lips kept moving in silent prayer; in tears we embraced, and parted. I ran off as fast as I could; and, when about to turn a corner in the road where he would lose sight

of me, I looked back and saw him still standing with head uncovered where I had left him—gazing after me. Waving my hat in adieu, I was round the corner and out of sight in an instant. But my heart was too full and sore to carry me further, so I darted into the side of the road and wept for a time. Then, rising up cautiously, I climbed the dyke to see if he yet stood where I had left him, and just at that moment I caught a glimpse of him climbing the dyke and looking out for me. He did not see me, and after he had gazed eagerly in my direction for a while he got down, set his face towards home, and began to return, his head still uncovered, and his heart, I felt sure, still rising in prayers for me. I watched through blinding tears, till his form faded from my gaze, and then, hastening on my way, vowed deeply and oft, by the help of God, to live and act so as never to grieve or dishonour such a father and mother as he had given me.[2]

As Paton's testimony points out, it is not wrong for us to mourn the good things—and good relationships—that we are being asked to leave. But clinging to Jesus requires that we follow him and entrust our future and theirs to his care while we strive to keep stride with our Lord, neither falling behind nor running ahead.

Friend, as you leave, may you grieve well that which is left behind and cling tightly to the One who holds you and your future.

DISCUSS AND REFLECT

1. Who will be the hardest people to leave? What are the ways that you've seen the Lord's kindness to you in those relationships? How will you express your gratitude to those individuals?

2. If you're married, what are ways that you can care for your spouse as he or she prepares to leave? If you have children, what are ways that you can proactively care for your kids together?

3. What are the various ways that the Lord has confirmed your ministry assignment? What are the Scripture passages and conversations that have encouraged you along the way?

CHAPTER 3

Identity and Task

Jeff Kelly

From the General Editor

I (MATT) HAVE the privilege of having known Jeff Kelly for more than a decade. We went to seminary together, deployed overseas together, and served in the same country for several years together. Jeff is a dear friend, a wise and kind shepherd, and a seasoned leader.

As a friend, I have found Jeff to be a brother who will speak with charity, conviction, and compassion into some of the most difficult aspects of life. He is that kind of sharp iron that sharpens the iron of his brothers (Prov. 27:17). As a co-laborer, I see in Jeff a faithful, indefatigable, servant of King Jesus. His energies appeared limitless to those looking on and his capacities outstripped most of the people with whom he worked on the field. And as a missiologist, I see in Jeff an abiding wisdom, biblically grounded strategy, and a passion for God's glory among the nations. Watching what the Lord continues to do through things that he used Jeff to build and launch is truly a joy.

As you read Jeff's words, it is my prayer that you would sense that they come from a walk of faith that has been tried, tested, and found true. I pray that you would hear and heed his impassioned summons to find your identity in Christ. And I pray that before you go, you would begin to implement his suggestions for how you would discipline yourself to cling to Christ the Rock amidst the trials and struggles that lay ahead.

INEFFECTIVE AND INSUFFICIENT

Gazing into the campfire that cool night in Limuru, Kenya, my brother touched a nerve. I can still remember the question the veteran missionary asked. I was a rookie language student on a retreat during my first year on the field. His question highlighted the enormity of the task: "What level of language will you need to accomplish the ministry you're aiming for?"[3]

Without needing to pause to think about it, I immediately knew my answer. My crosshairs had been trained on the goal of making disciples, planting a church, and raising up future pastors. To do so, I would need to aim well beyond mere conversational Arabic.

If I was to accomplish this goal with biblical faithfulness, I had *a lot* of work in front of me.

For one thing, pursuing this goal required a singular focus and commitment to language acquisition. And it came with some specific changes to my environment and expectations of myself. I was no longer living in the States, in a context I knew and could navigate. My days were no longer spent reaping the tangible rewards of productive ministry. The ability I once had to finish a hard day of work and celebrate concrete output was a thing of the past.

No, back in Jordan lay the harsh reality of my own inabilities. Any progress was slow, and headway was negligible. Staring at my Arabic notebook filled with غs, عs, and ضs, my own inadequacies were daily—even hourly—looming in front of my face. No longer could I pretend like I was sufficient. *My* capacity, *my* efficiency, *my* competence, and *my* "accomplishments" were *not* fulfilling and *not* impressive as I sputtered through simple sentences like a child.

PERSONAL IDENTITY AND THE MISSIONARY LIFE

Brother, as you are getting ready to engage in the same process of cross-cultural missions, I wonder where your heart will go when you face this same type of trial? I suspect you'll almost certainly encounter this stripping down of your own proficiencies. Maybe you'll face this in language. Maybe it will be in trying to avoid cultural offenses. Or maybe for you it will be in trying to make friends in a new culture. The question isn't whether the reality of an unrewarding slog is in front of you. Rather, the question is what you will do when you hit it.

Having watched many missionaries come to the field over the years, responses are varied. Generally, these experiences of role deprivation and identity stress are more acute for us men. For some, finding out you are not enough may lead you to turn around and go home. (At times, this may actually be the godly choice!) For others, a high pain tolerance will keep you on the field, but profound discouragement, disillusion, and frustration will become regrettable companions.

For others still, I fear you may have my default impulse. Facing this stripping away you'll double down and work harder to prove yourself. You'll work past the apparent incompetence, and then toil until you can stand up proudly behind the visible progress you've made in the missionary task. And as you do, you'll risk finding your identity in what you *do,* despite spreading a faith that is based on what's been *done.* You'll risk spiritual suicide.

Isn't there a better way? Is there hope that we can counter our patent insufficiencies without simply working to prove ourselves? The answer is a resounding yes! I believe Scripture offers powerful resources for dealing with the inevitable discovery that the task is beyond us. If I may, I would love to share some reflections on a passage that has been particularly helpful to me as I have considered these challenges in my own experience on the field:

> I have been crucified with Christ. It is no longer I who live, but Christ who lives in me. (Gal. 2:20a ESV)

Can I ask you a favor? Would you go back up to that verse and read it again slowly?

If this verse is true—and it is—then you are dead to yourself, but as you are united with Christ, you are enlivened by him. The most true, beautiful, and profound aspects about who you are, then, are found in the One to whom you are united.

Christian, you are who you are not because of what you do or do not do, but because you are in Christ.

I'm convinced the Christian doctrine of union with Christ is one of the most underutilized—and yet profoundly transformational—biblical doctrines not only for understanding our

IDENTITY AND TASK

salvation, but for living out the Christian life. If you are a believer, you are *in* Christ. Christ has not merely died for you, but he has united himself *to* you. As Calvin wrote, he has "ingrafted [us] into his body, [making us] participants not only in all his benefits but also in himself."[4] (If that sentence didn't make you tremble, you should probably read it again!) This means that his ability, strength, identity, and obedience are all now yours.

Consider just how profound this is for Paul in Galatians 2:20a (ESV): "I have been crucified with Christ. It is no longer I who live, but Christ who lives in me." When Paul looks at his life, he understands himself to be so profoundly united to Christ in his death that it is no longer Paul that is living. Think about that. This unsettling death to Paul's own identity couldn't be more radical!

Not only did Paul die with Christ, but now he says, "Christ lives in me." Paul's identity is now swallowed up with Christ living through him. Paul doesn't merely have an upgraded motivation for what he does. It's not like he was previously running empty on low-grade fuel and now he has a full tank of high-octane. No, Christ has given him a whole new vehicle.

The cash value for this profound truth in the missionary task cannot be overstated. When faced with our own inadequacies and enduring challenges on the field, understanding our union with Christ in our obedience shapes both our stability and our progress. Our stability turns rock-solid as the ballast beneath our ship is no longer our own self-perception. We are in Christ and we have nothing more to prove (1 John 4:10).

But this stability we enjoy as "in Christ" people is not idle; it also shapes our progress. We now have the resources to obey through the power of Christ at work in us (Eph. 3:20). The task he has sent us to do, he has the authority to accomplish, and has promised his very presence will go with us (Matt. 28:20).

Too often in my early years, my work and identity showed a heart that didn't *really* believe Jesus when he said, "you can do nothing without me" (John 15:5). Sure, I believed it in principle, but I didn't fully live it out. *My* effort was too often at the center. My gaze of my obedience wasn't always firmly fixed in faith to the union with Christ that was already mine. I wish I had embedded this reorienting perspective deeper into my heart even before I left for the Middle East. If I'm being honest, I still need to better apply it now, even as I write this!

If you're reading this book, I assume you are still on the front end of your life as a missionary. If you are to survive the tumult of entering a new culture and engaging in the missionary task, then you need to cultivate and enlarge this faith-filled consciousness of and dependence on your union with Christ. Before you can serve Christ well you must be convinced that your identity is established and secure in Christ and not determined by what you do for him. Let me offer four practical suggestions for how to do this.

COMMUNE WITH CHRIST

Before you go, you must first *know* Christ. Now, it may seem obvious that you should know Christ before you endeavor to serve him. And I pray that any church that would commission you as a missionary has already affirmed that you know Christ as Savior. But the knowledge of Christ I am talking about here is the intimate knowledge of the One who indwells you—the One who is your life. This is the experiential and existential knowledge of walking with Christ as one walks through life with an old friend. It's that close affinity, that dear kinship, which marked Enoch as he was known for walking with the Lord (Gen. 5:24). I wonder, does that typify you?

Brother, if you are to ground your identity in being in Christ, you must commune with Christ. And if you are intending your days to be dedicated to ministry, you must develop the habits of doing so daily. Letting your soul take delight in him must have already become your habit, your practice, and your daily joy. Learn to run regularly to the fountain of his presence until that path becomes well-trodden.

As you develop these reflexes, Christ and your connection to him will become more real to you than any task that is ever set in front of you. His person, his presence, his real and true existence will be more immediate to you than anything else. You will come to see and savor him until your eyes of faith have greater acuity than your eyes of sight. And as you know him and his goodness with increasing intimacy, you will also know the incredible reality of his approval of you that is independent of your productivity for him.

Practically, this means you must commune with Christ by giving yourself to prayer, Scripture reading, and gathering with your church. These are the means that Christ ordinarily uses to commune with his people. This means that before you begin the task of missions, you must be busy in the task of mining gold from the riches of the Word yourself. Before you direct others to Christ, you must direct your own soul to him through time spent on your knees. Before you gather other new believers together, you must yourself know the joy of meeting with Christ through his gathered body.

In the lived experience of your life, can you say with Paul that your life consists of and is defined by "Christ who lives in me" (Gal. 2:20 ESV)?

If you can't, when engaged in the task, your danger will be profound. It is possible that you were formerly tempted to place your identity in what you knew and could produce in your pre-missionary setting. If that is you, when your previous culture, previous language, and previous fruitfulness vanish, your soul will seek solace in reestablishing what you *do*, not in remembering who you *are*. Your joy will rise and fall with every victory and every battle. If you fail to commune with Christ, it will be the challenges and struggles that you face whose reality you will fixate on instead of the firm foundation of who Christ is and who you are in him.

In sum, your knowledge of Christ and Christ in you must be most real to you. As Richard B. Gaffin Jr. writes: "For those who are 'in Christ,' this union or solidarity is all-encompassing, extending in fact from eternity to eternity, from what is true of [you] 'before the creation of the world' to [your] still future glorification."[5] Brother, regardless of how long you stay overseas, your task in missions will one day end. But your union with Christ will never end. Let me urge you to build your life on this enduring rock.

UNDERSTAND WHAT CHRIST HAS DONE

A second, related piece of advice is to drink deeply from the well of Christ's accomplishment. If you want to enjoy the stability

IDENTITY AND TASK

and ability that come through your union with Christ, you must not only commune with Christ now, but you must also keenly understand what Christ has completed. Reflecting on my time preparing for the field, I have no regrets for any time I spent deepening my understanding of all that Christ accomplished in my salvation. Let me encourage you to do the same.

One way to help you grow in your depth of appreciation for the gospel is by reading well on the atonement. Explore the riches of the cross and become well acquainted with all that has happened in your redemption. Consider picking up a classic like John Murray's *Redemption: Accomplished and Applied* or John Stott's *The Cross of Christ*. Study your New Testament well, perhaps doing a deep dive into Romans or Hebrews. Consider doing a study like this with a friend from your local church to further ensure you see fresh insights into the fullness of the gospel.

I suspect that for most, the advice of understanding more of the gospel may not feel very practical or concrete. After all, you probably wouldn't be reading this book if you didn't already care profoundly about the gospel. However, when you consider your identity on the field, there is a direct relationship between how thoroughly you understand what Christ *has done* and how much you are controlled by what you feel *you must do*.

You see, when Christ unites himself to you, he gives you all of his benefits. His righteousness accomplished in the gospel is now yours. His perfected obedience is now bestowed on you. His declaration of "It is finished" (John 19:30) is now declared over your life before the Father. There's nothing left for you to do.

But when you arrive on the field and you find yourself stymied before the massive task of missions, your fallen instincts to define yourself by what you do will speak louder than your well-founded principles. You must retrain your instincts. To the person who knows and truly understands what Christ has fully accomplished, any unfinished business that lays before him will seem relatively insignificant in terms of its effect upon his identity. But to the one who has mere surface-level knowledge of the gospel, and has not learned it like an old friend, will struggle. His instinct of needing to produce will constantly switch into performance-mode autopilot.

Learn the gospel and study it now better than you think you need to. Understand what Christ has done for you until it is the lens by which you view all your doing. The relationship between your gospel saturation and ministry preparation should be like an iceberg whose peak is visibly manifest above the surface in your ministry, but whose peace stretches miles below the waterline. Brother, take heart—all righteousness has been fulfilled and there's nothing left for you to do.

STUDY FAITHFULNESS APART FROM PROGRESS

A third piece of advice I would offer as you prepare to head into the challenge of overseas work is to study other examples of what one author calls, "a long obedience in the same direction."[6] In order to live through destabilizing circumstances with a security in your identity with Christ, you will be helped by examining the lives and ministries of others who have done the same. Be a student of those who have gone before you.

But don't just limit yourself to those who have been faithful and successful in the eyes of the world. Doggedly pursue those

IDENTITY AND TASK

who were faithful apart from visible progress. Pick up some missionary biographies and let their testimonies put steel in your backbone. Let their examples of dependency on Christ train you. Witness the life and ministry of workers like Adoniram Judson and walk beside him as he limps out of the death prison to find his dear Nancy passing away. Ride in the plane next to Elisabeth Elliot as she returns to the same jungle where her husband was speared. Climb a horse alongside David Brainerd as his body grows increasingly worn and tired from a brutal itinerant ministry. Hide in the tree with John Paton to listen to his reflections of sweet communion with his savior, divorced from any sense of worldly success. Listen as he testifies:

> Alone, yet not alone! If it be to glorify my God, I will not grudge to spend many nights alone in such a tree, to feel again my Saviour's spiritual presence, to enjoy His consoling fellowship. If thus thrown back upon your own soul, alone, all, all alone, in the midnight, in the bush, in the very embrace of death itself, have you a Friend that will not fail you then?[7]

Brother, before you go, take time to learn at the feet of such men and women. And as you do, you'll discover why the author of Hebrews not only recounts those who were victorious in faith (11:32–35a), but also those who were brought low in faith (11:35b–38). Discover God's beautiful design to use us, not because of the success we bring, but because of the One who has united himself to us. You will find that even though these forebearers in the faith and in the task had feet of clay, they lived confidently in the knowledge of their unshakable identity in the Lord.

CELEBRATE CHRIST AT WORK THROUGH OTHERS

Let me offer one final piece of advice for preparing for those disorienting days overseas. Before you ever step onto a plane, develop the muscle and reflex of celebrating Christ at work through others. Learn to be on the lookout for God's work *not* through your efforts, but through someone else's.

On our own, this ability is beyond us. Our hearts are naturally turned in on ourselves. We make much of what we're doing in an attempt to bolster our own confidence. Little do we realize, this actually makes us less secure, not more so.

But if Christ has truly united himself to you, you should have the confidence that you couldn't be any more valued than you are right now. This will free you up to look beyond yourself. Being found in him, you can radically appreciate what he is doing through those around you.

When you get to the field, applying this aspect of your union with Christ will be crucial. From day one, every person you meet will be more skilled at language, culture, and ministry than yourself. If you can't celebrate—and keep celebrating—what you witness in other missionaries, you'll miss out. If you can't humble yourself to recognize language skills that are better than your own, your growth will be stymied. And if you can't celebrate how God is working through the national church that is there, your ministry will be torpedoed.

But the stability of resting in Christ can be developed before you leave as you start now in being an extravagant voice of affirmation. Search out his grace in others. See how often you can find it in the lives of those around you. Make much of what might seem to be "small" successes in the lives of other brothers and sisters in your church. When you see someone who is living as one who is crucified with Christ, don't miss the chance to tell them. Develop these muscles now and don't wait. It will be good for you, for them, and for your future ministry.

IDENTIFYING WITH CHRIST

I left that campfire in Kenya and returned to Jordan, throwing myself into my work. I embraced the study, the ministry, and the painfully slow task of missions in a difficult environment. As I reflect on that season, while my own faith-filled obedience wasn't perfect, I suspect that a large measure of the stability I enjoyed was due to what the Lord had taught me about my identity in Christ. By God's grace alone, our family went on to spend more than a decade serving in the Middle East.

But for our family, this has not been where our story has ended. The day came when it was time for our family to return to the States.

Now I'm guessing if you're preparing to go for the long haul, the last thing you're thinking about is what it will be like to one day return. But it might surprise you to hear that the shock to your identity and the lessons you'll need are eerily similar returning as they were when arriving. The reason is that too often we can replace one earthly identity (productive minister) with another (long-term missionary).

Friend, finding yourself in Christ is the only true antidote. Wherever it's found, replace the idol of proving your own self-worth with the glorious freedom of being united to your Savior. Know him, commune with him, and glory in the beauty of your redemption. Only then will you have the ballast to meaningfully join in taking the gospel to the ends of the earth.

DISCUSS AND REFLECT

1. How well are you faithfully communing with Christ now? Does your life reflect a regular sweet fellowship with Christ in Scripture, prayer, and assembling in a local church? How can your communion grow?

2. Does your motivation for obedience rest in what Christ has already accomplished? In what ways do you find your worthiness in your own good works? How can you put this to death?

3. What biographies have you read of faithful missionaries? What should you read next?

CHAPTER 4

Integrity and Accountability

D. Scott Hildreth

From the General Editor

WHEN I (MATT) was a seminary student, I had the chance to study under Scott Hildreth in several classes. As a brother who exhibited a sharp mind, a missionary vision, and experience from the field, I was quickly inclined to listen to all that he had to say. Unbeknownst to Scott and his wife, my wife and I looked up to them as early examples of faithful missionaries whose lives and ministries were worthy of imitation.

As my studies continued, my opportunities to spend more time around Scott increased and my appreciation for his ministry, wisdom, and pastoral heart only grew. As an elder, professor, and missions expert, Scott has had many opportunities to walk closely with missionary candidates as they prepare to launch. He has also had the unfortunate experience of walking closely with missionaries who have been dismissed from the field for lack of personal integrity.

While the idea of falling into disqualifying sin might seem inconceivable as you consider launching into missionary service, the reality is that it seemed inconceivable to most of those who have succumbed to temptation. At the same time, Scott's chapter helpfully points out some of the seemingly less-egregious sins that persistently confront missionaries: laziness, inaccurate reports, and poor stewardship. Before you go, my prayer is that Scott's wise counsel and caution would be part of what the Lord uses to reveal the importance of your investment in your own integrity as a sent one.

A MINISTRY-SHAPING SENTENCE

"If you don't take care of your heart and your life, you will not stay on the field."

This sentence came from one of my first conversations with one of my supervisors soon after arriving on the mission field.

He continued: "You may not want to go home. Your wife and kids may not want to go home. You might cry all the way to the airport and be in tears when the plane lifts off. But I can promise you that missionaries who are not careful about the important parts of their lives do not survive on the mission field."

It is difficult to overstate the impact this conversation had on me. The fact that I remember it nearly twenty-five years later ought to speak to its importance; but more to the point, I have used this same talk with missionaries and mission students through the years. Successful missionary service requires a strong work ethic and moral integrity.

INTEGRITY AND ACCOUNTABILITY

I am a firm believer in the missionary call. In my experience, a clear call through the affirmation of a local church is often the factor that helps missionaries endure. When days are tough, nothing else motivates us to stick it out like the knowledge that the Lord has placed us in our current ministry assignment. However, it has also been my experience that a lack of integrity and accountability will destroy your missionary career, even if you have received a clear call from the Lord. This chapter will unpack why integrity is at the heart of successful missionary work. It will also provide some practical guidelines that will enable you to serve the Lord successfully for a long time.

THE MEASUREMENT ISSUE

Before we get into any of the specifics of this chapter, we need to acknowledge something about missionary work that exacerbates some of our problems with integrity: successful Christian ministry, including missionary work, is difficult to measure. The work is often slow, and measuring internal, qualitative change is challenging to assess. While this is not inherently problematic, it does have a bearing on our integrity and work ethic—both personally and externally.

As biblical evidence for this, consider these thoughts:

- Ephesians 4:13 says that ministry is not complete until all reach unity of the faith and maturity that is measured by Christlikeness.

- In Colossians 1:28, Paul says his ministry continues until he can present everyone mature, or perfect, in Christ.

On the one hand, these passages can be encouraging. They remind us that the work is deeply spiritual and that such goals cannot be rushed. Furthermore, they encourage us to keep at the work for the long haul. And while Christlike perfection is the stated goal in these passages, they implicitly affirm that we are always people who are in process.

On the other hand, without obvious benchmarks to measure our efforts, we can become inattentive to diligent approaches to ministry. We can cite the vagueness of ministry progress as a way of sugarcoating laziness and a lack of intentionality. In ministry, where fruit is beyond our control, it is possible to blame God or others for the lack of growth when, in reality, we have settled into mediocrity. As missionaries, one way that we must display integrity and a strong work ethic is to maintain a genuine pursuit of personal spiritual growth. Because we often labor in anonymity, a lackadaisical approach to watching our lives can lead us to collapse, and our ministries can crumble before anyone recognizes a problem exists. Our spiritual health is not merely about producing—it is an issue of integrity and stewardship.

Beyond the brief references cited above, it might be helpful to consider Paul's more extensive treatment of the topic as he writes to the Thessalonian church in 2 Thessalonians 3:6–13:

> Now we command you, brothers and sisters, in the name of our Lord Jesus Christ, to keep away from every brother or sister who is idle and does

INTEGRITY AND ACCOUNTABILITY

not live according to the tradition received from us. For you yourselves know how you should imitate us: We were not idle among you; we did not eat anyone's food free of charge; instead, we labored and toiled, working night and day, so that we would not be a burden to any of you. It is not that we don't have the right to support, but we did it to make ourselves an example to you so that you would imitate us. In fact, when we were with you, this is what we commanded you: "If anyone isn't willing to work, he should not eat." For we hear that there are some among you who are idle. They are not busy but busybodies. Now we command and exhort such people by the Lord Jesus Christ to work quietly and provide for themselves. But as for you, brothers and sisters, do not grow weary in doing good.

In this passage, Paul gives two important considerations related to ministry integrity: a warning against laziness and a call to endurance.

A WARNING AGAINST LAZINESS

The word translated as "idle" in verse 6 is the Greek word *ataktōs*. One commentator says that the best way to articulate the meaning of this word is to define it as "irresponsible behavior . . . freeloading, sponging."[8]

BEFORE YOU GO

For some unexplained reason, some Thessalonian Christians had embraced laziness as a lifestyle. Their behavior was so egregious that Paul felt it necessary to warn the church to avoid these people. New Testament scholar Gordon Fee has observed that Paul's warning is "the strongest language in the entire passage, indeed the entire letter."[9] As much as Paul would undoubtedly want the lazy folks to change, his letter addresses those who are not themselves lazy. He does not want the innocent to be tarnished by their fellow church members' bad habits or poor reputations.

To be clear, there is no spiritual virtue in embracing the other end of the spectrum—being a workaholic. However, this passage warns all of us about the spiritual danger of laziness. Contrary to idleness, Paul provides his own missionary lifestyle as an example of how one should work with diligence in order to reinforce the integrity of the message. He knows his behavior reflects on the credibility of the gospel.

As a missionary, your lifestyle will differ significantly from the nationals you live among. While they go to work each day, the "job" you have been sent to do is ministry. Even if your responsibilities include tasks that mirror businesspeople in your community, gospel work requires intentional labor if you are to be faithful to discharge the duties given to you by your sending church and, ultimately, by the Lord. As we noted above, the circumstances in which we minister usually provide significant freedom and flexibility. It is possible to be lazy for a while before anyone notices. However, this verse reminds us that our labor is in the name of our Lord Jesus, and we work to please him, whether anyone else notices or not.

INTEGRITY AND ACCOUNTABILITY

AN EXHORTATION TOWARD ENDURANCE

A follow-up to Paul's warning about laziness is his challenge to continue in the work, even when it is difficult. If anyone knows about the hardships of being a missionary, Paul is the guy. He reminds the Christians at Corinth of these hardships in 2 Corinthians 11:26–28. He says:

> . . . I faced dangers from rivers, dangers from robbers, dangers from my own people, dangers from Gentiles, dangers in the city, dangers in the wilderness, dangers at sea, and dangers among false brothers; toil and hardship, many sleepless nights, hunger and thirst, often without food, cold, and without clothing. Not to mention other things, there is the daily pressure on me: my concern for all the churches.

Paul encourages the Thessalonians: "*do not grow weary in doing good*" (2 Thess. 3:13, emphasis mine). Ministry is hard, and it is easy to find a reason to quit. Success on the mission field demands a work ethic that endures hardships. Missionary service is not a solo enterprise. We serve in relationships with our church, sending agency, team, and national partners. We cannot just give up; others depend on our labor for their success.

MISSIONARY INTEGRITY AND YOUR SEXUAL PURITY

As we reflect on integrity in our work, we also need to look at another warning Paul issued to the Thessalonian church:

BEFORE YOU GO

> For this is God's will, your sanctification: that you keep away from sexual immorality, that each of you knows how to control his own body in holiness and honor, not with lustful passions, like the Gentiles, who don't know God. . . . For God has not called us to impurity but to live in holiness. (1 Thess. 4:3–5, 7)

Okay men, move in here real close. Let's talk about another area that too many missionaries fail to take seriously: your personal purity. Pornography and sexual immorality have derailed far more ministries than we care to reflect on. Along with the decimation of the work, failure in this area will also cause significant shame and devastation in your relationship with your wife, children, and ministry partners. And at its core, it is a rejection of your Savior's call to holy living. Furthermore, it gives an opportunity for the Evil One to mock our Lord, the gospel, and the church.

Paul's words offer us a perfect warning here. Let me touch on two ways that integrity requires us to pursue purity with intentional and devoted effort as missionaries. First, we need a reminder that our purity is God's desire. Second, we must recognize that our purity reflects our devotion and calling.

Our Purity Is God's Will

Dietrich Bonhoeffer observed that allowing lust to overpower us is like fanning a smoldering ember into a blazing flame. Lust controls our thinking and our passions. What we previously understood to be wrong is easily justified. He wrote: "God is quite

INTEGRITY AND ACCOUNTABILITY

unreal to us . . . Satan does not fill us with hatred of God, but forgetfulness of God."[10]

When tempted to look at pornography or consider engaging in sexual immorality, we try to convince ourselves that it's "Okay." We tell ourselves that God understands. However, Paul is quite clear that sexual immorality is never God's will. I want to plead with you, brother, to flee the tempting whispers of our Enemy in this area. It is likely that you will have passing thoughts like:

> "I have given up so much to be here serving the Lord, so I have earned a little pleasure."
>
> "What is the big deal with this victimless indulgence?"
>
> "There are so many stressors, and this is a harmless stress release."
>
> "This compromise will stop me from giving into bigger temptations."

Putting these ridiculous excuses in print surely demonstrates that they are worthy of immediate dismissal. But in the heat of temptation, you may admit they seem much more rational, if not more powerful. Brother, your sexual purity is a part of your pursuit of holiness. It is always God's will to develop holiness in you. So do not give in to the lies and temptations that compromising in private is ever a "small thing."

Our Purity Reflects Our Spiritual Devotion and Missionary Call

In addition to its effect on our private spiritual life, pursuing sexual holiness will also bear fruit in our ministry. Our missionary life places us in cultures that express and practice sexuality differently. Because of this, we will likely find ourselves bombarded with images, invitations, and even opportunities we are unprepared to handle. It may be true that "everyone in our context is doing it." But it is not true that culturally accepted, unbiblical compromises are allowable. God has placed us in spiritually dark places in order to bring light and to be his witnesses.

Church historians have pointed out that early Christians were often mocked because of their sexual ethics. However, their elevated morality also served as a distinguishing feature that drew Romans out of their paganism to the gospel. Though the culture celebrated debauchery, even the opponents of early Christians admitted that these people following a biblical lifestyle had a positive impact on society.

Furthermore, beyond the actual sin itself, the destructive effects of such compromise on our marriage and family would certainly impact our ministry. I can't help but remember one Sunday, my pastor was preaching on the importance of purity, and he shared the following reflection from a letter written to himself as a reminder of the high cost of sexual immorality:

> If I had an affair, I would cause untold hurt to [my wife], and I would have to endure the loss of her respect and trust, and might forever forfeit my relationship to her.

INTEGRITY AND ACCOUNTABILITY

I would cause deep hurt and confusion in [my kids], who may never understand why I traded a close relationship with them for a thrill. Yes, I could likely stay involved in their lives. My relationship with them would never be the same.

I would bring shame on my mother and father.

I would bring endless judgment on the woman I committed adultery with. Her life would be forever labeled by this encounter. If she had kids, I would be the biggest stumbling block for them learning to trust in Jesus.

I would confuse and discourage many in their walk of faith.

I would cause shame to you, my church family.

I would give easy fodder to all those searching for reasons to mock Christianity and say it is phony and untrue.

I would follow in the footsteps of men I know whose immorality forfeited their ministry and stained the name of the church—men you've heard of.

Most important, I would grieve my Lord and Savior and one day I will have to look him in the face and explain why—after all he had given to me, after all the blessing and beauty he had put into my life—I had to have something else.[11]

Men, let us determine to handle our sexual desires in a Christlike manner. Let holiness and our sanctification be the benchmarks in this area of our lives.

MAINTAINING INTEGRITY AND ACCOUNTABILITY FOR LONG, HEALTHY MINISTRY

The measurements for ministry success differ from most vocations. The work can feel tedious and unrewarding. This feeling of endless toil can make us vulnerable to laziness and bad habits. Some of these actions seem inconsequential, but small compromises in our integrity can chip away at the work and at our sanctification. I want to conclude this chapter with four practical suggestions that will set you up for a long, healthy ministry.

1. Do Important Little Things

The missionary life includes some monumental moments. We are called and commissioned. We pack our bags and settle into a new home. We share our faith; some believe and are baptized. Yet, despite these significant milestones, it is a mistake to presume life and ministry consist of major accomplishments and activities.

Though notable, these public events and mountaintop moments are not the foundation for successful ministry. In fact, if we are not careful, the allure of newsletter-worthy activities can actually be detrimental. As with most disciplines, if you want long-term missionary success, prioritize the little things and give

INTEGRITY AND ACCOUNTABILITY

yourself to them diligently. Here is a list of some of those "little things:"

- Dedicate daily time to reading the Word and praying.
- Shepherd your family by reserving time for them as individuals and as a family.
- Invest in learning the local language and work at it diligently.
- Set goals for meeting new people and forming friendships with locals.
- Learn the rhythms of your city and investigate why things are the way they are.
- _____ (Fill in the blank with your own small step.)

These are the actions you can reasonably ignore, and no one will call you on it. But in time, if you neglect them, your foundation will be irreparably weakened. To this point, I love these words from Paul David Tripp:

> The little moments of life are profoundly important precisely because they are the little moments that we live in and that form us. This is where I think "Big Drama Christianity" gets us into trouble. It can cause us to devalue the significance of the little moments of life and the "small-change." . . . You see, the character of a life is not set in two or three dramatic moments, but in 10,000 little moments. The character that was

formed in those little moments is what shapes how you respond to the big moments of life.[12]

2. Maintain Your Walk with the Lord

One of the leaders in our missionary training warned: "If you pick up your language book before you pick up your Bible, you are already in trouble." Serving as a missionary includes many important tasks. However, none are more important than your relationship with the Lord. Jesus reminded his disciples: "I am the vine; you are the branches. The one who remains in me and I in him produces much fruit, because you can do nothing without me" (John 15:5).

Nurturing a deep and growing relationship with the Lord is a lifeline for ministry. Our time reading the Scriptures and praying keeps us connected to Jesus as the source of life. My wife tells the story of being deep in culture shock; she was angry, scared, and even ashamed. Yet, she'd pick up the Bible and read it every day. Later she reflected on that season and her devotional life in the darkness: "I didn't get a lot out of it. Most days, it was like the words didn't make sense, and my prayers stopped at the ceiling. But I knew Jesus was my only source for strength, and I was afraid that if I ever skipped a day, I might never pick the Bible up again."

Eventually, the Lord led her out of the darkness, and she had a tremendous ministry. However, she often looks back to those early days on the mission field as transformative. They serve as a constant reminder that doing the little things and practicing simple disciplines kept her from falling.

INTEGRITY AND ACCOUNTABILITY

3. Do the Job They Sent You to Do

Missionaries are commissioned by their churches and mission organizations to a task. Each job is different, but when we are sent, they entrust us with significant responsibility. We may do the job in relative isolation or anonymity, but this doesn't lessen the importance of the trust given.

It is easy to get distracted on the mission field. Other missionaries may have an assignment you wish was yours. You may be convinced that you could do the other job better. There is also the continual siren call of popular time-wasters like excessive play, social media engagement, perfectionism, or time with the ex-pat community. Any of these—and we know the list could go on and on—will keep us from fulfilling our purpose.

Someone determined this specific role was important. From a missionary perspective, success equals the fulfillment of God's plan for the nations. From an earthly perspective, our diligence means maximizing the money, prayers, and resources of many men, women, and children. Any experienced missionary knows there are seasons of excitement and seasons of boredom. Some days feel like we are pushing a boulder up a mountain, while others feel like it is crushing us on its way down. The challenge is to be faithful to the task and to live responsibly before the Lord and others so that the specific challenge we've been given can be accomplished.

4. Establish and Welcome Accountability Structures

Finally, let me remind you that you do not stop needing the accountability of your brothers and sisters just because you got on a plane. Even as a missionary in vocational ministry, you are a person who needs others in your fight for holiness. Just like back home, an accountability group is vital to your spiritual health. But it is only as effective as you allow it to be.[13]

We are all "smart enough" to manipulate the situation, avoiding prying eyes and probing questions. But we should never forget that *blind spots*, by definition, means there are things that we don't see. Sure, it can be embarrassing and painful to invite someone (or a group of people) to examine your life. But the consequences of failure are too great to think you can do it alone.

I'm reminded of the story of David and his sin with Bathsheba and the ultimate murder of Uriah. The writer of 2 Samuel is careful to point out that the king was alone and isolated (see 11:1–27). David sent his friends away and ignored the warnings of his servants. At the moment of great need, this man who had written about the Lord as our Shepherd (Ps. 23) seems to have forgotten who he was. Our challenge is to put into place whatever accountability structures we need so that our lives and ministries are long and successful.

AVOIDING SHIPWRECK

My family served nearly a decade overseas before God led us back to the United States where we have been equipping others for the task. Of course, we were sad to leave, and over the years, we have prayed about returning to the mission field. However, our present ministries continue fulfilling the missionary passion and calling God planted in our hearts many years ago.

In the last twenty-five years, I have known hundreds of men and women who serve the Lord in hard places. Some see tremendous fruit, while others spend years planting seeds and breaking hardened soil. It has been the joy of my life to equip and cheer them on as they go.

Unfortunately, I have also discovered that the words of my field supervisor are true. I have known some who neglected their private lives and allowed their integrity to be undermined by a hundred little compromises along the way. Some didn't develop the necessary missionary skills for survival, and some didn't nurture their Christian walk. In time, their careers have been cut short. Some have returned to the United States in shame, some in anger. Others have simply quit before the final collapse. Their calling had not changed, and the urgency of the need that drew them to the mission field still exists. But their failure to maintain the basic disciplines ultimately ended their ministries prematurely.

Brothers, if you are to be faithful to the end, cling to the Spirit. Discipline yourself toward integrity in work and purity. Our social media feeds are full of men and women who are not finishing ministry well. But we can be sure there are literally thousands of men and women like you laboring and walking in faithfulness. Our prayer is that you count yourself among these saints who serve for "an audience of one" and anticipate hearing: "Well done, good and faithful servant!" (Matt. 25:21).

BEFORE YOU GO

DISCUSS AND REFLECT

1. What is your greater temptation: perfectionism or procrastination? How do these negatively influence your ministry work habits?

2. What "little things" are you most tempted to neglect? What plan can you put in place to hold yourself accountable?

3. How are you feeding your sexual lust? (Don't skip this question!) Write a letter reminding you what this will cost you if you continue.

4. What is your ministry role? Describe what success looks like. What do you need to do now to move toward this goal?

CHAPTER 5

Serving Well as a Team

Josh Bowman

From the General Editor

IT IS A great privilege to get to work with people for whom you care deeply and whom you respect greatly. In this season of life, I (Matt) am enjoying that privilege in getting to work with Josh Bowman as we teach Missions and Theology at Cedarville University. Josh and I have known each other since 2015 when we began our doctoral program together, and our friendship has deepened as we have been colleagues at Cedarville since 2018.

Not only does Josh have seventeen years of experience serving in various fields as a missionary with a pastoral heart and church-centered vision, he also wrote his dissertation on the idea of biblical partnership—an idea inextricably related to team. All of these aspects of Josh's ministry made him a beloved team leader during his time overseas. I have personally heard former teammates of his comment that he was the team leader they wished that everyone could have.

For all these reasons, Josh is well-equipped to write this chapter offering advice on how to be a member of a missionary team. Though you will commonly hear people say that team is the number-one reason that people leave the mission field, it does not have to be that way. Before you go, take Josh's advice to heart as you prepare to integrate into, form, or even lead a team of those who are seeking to make Jesus famous among the nations.

WHO ARE THESE PEOPLE?

We knew we were young. We knew we would need some guidance and encouragement in our ministry. We would need teammates to live life with us, love our four children, and labor side by side to take the gospel to the nations. So before God confirmed in our hearts the place that he was sending my wife, Amy, and me to serve as missionaries, we began praying for a mentor and team. Little did I know that the guest from Zambia who "randomly" spoke to my missions class in seminary would be the answer to those prayers.

When we first arrived at the airport in Zambia, we were overwhelmed by signs that said, "Welcome home," and missionaries asking our son to call them aunt and uncle. While exhausted from international travel with an infant, it did not take long to recognize Lusaka, Zambia, was not Jacksonville, Florida, and these strangers were not people we recognized familiarly as family. A few months later, this mission family gathered to celebrate Thanksgiving. Nearly fifty adults and children crammed into the conference room for the potluck celebration. Most knew one another well because they had forged deep friendships over the years of missionary service together. I was the new guy, overwhelmed and longing for the small family gathering at my parents' home that never exceeded ten to twelve people. Initially, this was all too much.

Something changed in the subsequent months as ministry and life circumstances led us to depend on our missionary team. In our rural village, our vision of team expanded beyond other Americans to include national brothers and sisters who were vital partners in life and ministry. Part of what drove us into deeper relationships with our missionary team and national partners was our genuine neediness. We came to serve, but we needed logistical help in finding a home and ways to learn the language. We needed help with medical decisions as my son began to have seizures, and my wife was pregnant. I had been to seminary, but needed my team leader to model ministry and mentor me through my first steps. Our youthful zeal and neediness were met with kindness, direction, and accountability, thereby shaping the next seventeen years of our missionary journey in both Zambia and South Asia.

PHILIPPIANS 1: PARTNERSHIP IN THE GOSPEL

Joy and thanksgiving characterize the letter that the apostle Paul wrote to the church at Philippi. Despite his imprisonment, Paul rejoiced because of the encouragement of these believers and, ultimately, because the gospel was advancing. Healthy teams on the mission field do not exclusively focus on either interpersonal relationships or the missionary task at the expense of the other. In Philippians 1, we see how brothers and sisters striving side by side in gospel ministry experience personal joy through faithful gospel witness, resulting in gospel advance.

Paul describes the deep, warm relationship he cherished with the saints at Philippi as he says, "I have you in my heart" (Phil. 1:7). He continues: "God is my witness, how deeply I miss all of you with the affection of Christ Jesus" (v. 8). He consistently prays for these friends. He knows his presence with these believers will result in their "progress and joy in the faith" (v. 25). Paul knows these friends not simply through shallow acquaintance or connection through shared-but-shallow interests, like following the same sports team. On a much deeper level, his relationship with these believers was forged through the fire of persecution and the sweat of gospel ministry.

In the context of Paul's itinerant ministry, "team" took many forms, but it always meant "partnership in the gospel" (v. 5). Team for Paul was not merely a relationship of mere acquaintance or passive proximity. Team did not stop at fellowship around a shared meal or spending time in leisure and pleasure. Instead, team referred to co-laborers who both defended and confirmed the gospel despite a hostile culture (v. 7). Furthermore, it meant supporting one another despite the risk and reality of imprisonment for speaking the message of Christ (vv. 7, 13–14).

Paul believed that his life, his relationships, and even his freedom served the greater cause of proclaiming and advancing the kingdom of God. Amazingly, Paul saw his imprisonment as a positive because it caused the Philippian church to be bolder and speak the truth "fearlessly" (v. 14). Others might condemn gospel teachers motivated by selfish ambition, but not Paul. He was content to be afflicted, rejoicing that "Christ is proclaimed" (v. 18).

Team for Paul meant serving and putting the interest of others above himself. He modeled this by seeking to bless this church with his presence, instead of the more desirable outcome of being with Christ through death (vv. 23–24).

Paul understood that unity was a priority because he understood that unity was, first and foremost, a reality. Despite the differences in personality, disposition, and gifting between Paul and his co-laborers in the gospel, their essential unity was already established by Christ redeeming them in all their diversity into one family, into one body. Therefore, Paul's encouragement to his partners to pursue unity was not grounded in the hope of establishing an interpersonal, relational unification. Instead, it was grounded in the fact that this unity is already true in Christ.

Satan desires nothing less than to sow relational discord among missionary teams while simultaneously seeking to distract and derail the mission. Missionaries who thrive long-term on the mission field are usually convictional about methodology and thick-skinned about hardships. These traits are needed to survive and thrive cross-culturally, but may also lead to conflict with other team members.

However, Paul's focus on unity does not cause him to pause over disagreements between co-laborers. In Philippians 4, Paul entreats two faithful women who labored with him in ministry to agree and reconcile (vv. 2–3). He didn't doubt their status as believers since he states their "names are in the book of life" (v. 3). He reminds the church it is their job to facilitate the repair of this relationship by holding them together. Typical teams will have conflict, but they should also fight for unity because they are fellow workers submitting to the same King and participating in a joint mission.

PRACTICAL IDEAS FOR TEAMING WELL

1. Theology: Ensure that the foundation for your team is strong by aligning theologically.

As we see in Paul's letters, he believes that theology matters. As we saw above, Paul's challenge to two disputing sisters in the faith rests on his theological convictions regarding salvation creating a fundamental unity. Thus, theology matters because what you believe directly impacts your actions. For men today, theology matters when considering placing an engagement ring on your girlfriend's hand. It matters when considering a local church to join. And from my experience on various teams, I can attest that theology matters on missionary teams as you communicate the gospel in spiritually dark places and devise a missionary strategy for forming healthy disciples and churches together.

Teams should, of course, agree about foundational issues such as the key elements of the gospel (1 Cor. 15:1–5) and the nature and authority of Scripture (2 Tim. 3:16–17). A team that does not agree about the eternal condition of those without Christ is obviously headed toward dangerous waters. Possibly less apparent is how alignment in issues regarding the church impact team unity and partnership with local churches on the field. A team divided on topics such as church membership requirements, church leadership, the meaning of the Lord's Supper, church discipline, and the proper mode and candidates for baptism will lead to internal team division and external confusion with national partners.

We live in a day when nondenominationalism thrives. Doctrinal distinctives are often ignored or eroded in favor of a broader pan-evangelicalism. This is especially true on the mission field, where we realize that the need to engage the lost trumps our need to split hairs over theological minutiae. While we might recognize brothers and sisters of different doctrinal persuasions as believers, we can simultaneously recognize that forming a missionary team with them might be unwise. For example, it will be nearly impossible for a church-planting team to simultaneously have a member who believes infant baptism is proper while another convictionally holds to believers' baptism only.

Conflict, confusion, and division are unnecessarily sown when team members don't align theologically. Partnering more narrowly not only saves the team from some internal squabbling, but also saves young believers from having to sort out for themselves theological disagreements between those who have come to teach them. By God's grace, you will set precedents for new groups of believers that will continue to grow and impact future generations with the gospel—so may we never bring confusion or disunity to new believers!

Theological differences will impact the goals, priorities, strategies, and methods a team adopts to guide their daily work. Objectives, goals, and action plans all flow from how we understand God, his mission, and our partnership in God's mission. For example, should a team mainly focus on evangelism and work to harvest souls among receptive people groups? Should church strengthening and preparation of national pastors be the main work? Should meeting physical, educational, and general humanitarian needs be the priority of team members? The point is not to answer these questions for you, but to show you how practical decisions about cross-cultural ministry will flow from your theological convictions. Therefore, theological alignment on a team is crucial to your unity in relationships and success in the task.

A practical takeaway should be to make sure you have the theological education necessary to fulfill God's calling on your life. Minimally, you should know, affirm, and be competent to teach the doctrinal statement of your sending church and your agency. Additionally, you should have conversations with your team leader and missions' leadership to ensure you are on the same page. This may mean walking through a doctrinal statement together followed by conversations about how this theology translates to everyday ministry, strategy decisions, and interactions with nationals. Finally, remember that theological alignment aims for alignment on core doctrines without expecting complete uniformity on every issue.

2. Relationship: Pray, play, and share life with one another.

The labor required of a missionary is seemingly endless. The pressing spiritual needs of the lost can be overwhelming. This perennial fact makes it necessary for missionary teams to love and care for one another as brothers and sisters before and beyond the fact that they are coworkers. Even though it requires time and energy that could be dedicated to external-facing field work, fostering and enjoying healthy relationships on a team does not impede gospel ministry. I would argue it is a catalyst. It actually makes you stronger, more resilient, and better able to cooperate. Laughing together about life, crying together about struggles, and sitting together in submission to the Word are simple, yet indispensable, elements of healthy team formation.

Paul was undoubtedly committed to gospel work, yet, in one letter, he writes about his commitment to share "not only the gospel," but something else. Honestly, this is striking as we reflect on what else he could add to the gospel. He says, "We cared so much for you that we were pleased to share with you not only the gospel of God but also our own lives, because you had become dear to us" (1 Thess. 2:8). Paul recognized that the most important message in the world was communicated by a messenger. Furthermore, the relationship between the messenger, his team, and gospel recipients was worth developing.

Our team meetings in both Zambia and South Asia involved the usual planning, prayers, training, and reports. After these important discussions, we all looked forward to the plates coming out for meals. After breaking bread, we often broke out cards and games that resulted in playing together late into the evenings. Our common calling brought us together, but we also worked hard to relax and de-stress. In Zambia, this meant coming out of our rural villages to meet in the capital every few months. In South Asia, this meant having the team stay late in our high-rise apartment complex to share stories, holidays, and birthdays.

To be honest, in a different setting back in America, some of our teammates would not naturally gravitate toward one another. Our personalities differed. Our interests were divergent. And we did have times when we disagreed on strategy or had conflicts that needed resolving. Feelings got hurt, apologies were given, and strategy decisions were debated. Yet, laughing together and loving one another kept disagreements in check and helped alleviate some natural tensions when relationships are merely transactional and formal.

Unquestionably, your teammates will be quirky and might drive you crazy sometimes. However, common convictions about the gospel and the task combined with a mutual commitment to love one another well can go a long way in mediating tensions. Team relationships are not merely about your preferences and what others can do for you. God has called you to do hard things, and running together provides encouragement and accountability to finish the race well.

Decide before you go that you will be a good teammate. By joining a team, you choose to partner with others with similar convictions and goals in God's mission. Your intentional development of interpersonal relationships within the team will be a blessing as you strive together in gospel ministry. It certainly was for my family and me.

3. Strategy/Task: Agree on and clearly communicate team goals, expectations, and strategies.

Theology and doctrine are not the only important aspects to consider when seeking team alignment. Before you select the movie on your international flight to your ministry location, you should be aware of and in agreement with your team's strategy. Please don't naively assume that because you agree to a broad theological creed, team members will automatically value the same methods or objectives. You should know what the team hopes to accomplish in the next few years and how they expect to work toward those goals. How would the team define and measure success?

SERVING WELL AS A TEAM

As a team leader, I wanted team members to arrive with theological conviction and missiological awareness. I also wanted them to learn about the local people and ministry context. Our team hoped that new members would be moldable and teachable. Those who thought they knew it all or wanted to fix the long-term missionaries' "broken strategies" before jet lag wore off made less-than-ideal teammates. Humility and a genuine desire to learn will go a long way.

As you begin to assess your particular role on the team, remember to include national partners in your ministry plans. Those with the greatest proximity to spiritually and physically needy people will best be able to help you assess the need and formulate ministry plans. Taking the time to learn the language and make genuine relationships is not a time-waster. Instead, committing to being a learner in these areas will make your impact and influence greater and more sustainable.

Appreciate the local believers and foreign missionaries who have blazed a trail and learned hard lessons. Ask about the challenges and obstacles they faced as you adapt to your new world. Ask them about their current strategy plan and overall team goals. Learn the history and adaptations they have made based on their experience. Assume as you listen that the Spirit of God has led them, and they are being faithful to their calling.

4. Role/Diversity: Utilize the gifts of every team member.

I'm not a big jigsaw puzzle fan. Still, I know that each puzzle piece should fit in its proper place in service of the big picture the puzzle intends to display. As a new team member, you must prayerfully discern where you fit into the work. This will differ based on your spiritual gifts, the members of your team, and the strength and needs of any existing local churches. Your work may be diverse and broad as you begin to engage in evangelism, discipleship, church formation, and leadership development. On the other hand, it is also possible that your work could be narrow, meeting a specific practical niche.

Whatever your role, it is critical you see both the overall team strategy and how your individual part complements and accomplishes the team's mission. Your gifts, ideas, and background may be wildly different from others on the team. You may be tempted to compare or feel like you don't have as much to contribute. Can I remind you of the image of the church as a body in Romans 12 and 1 Corinthians 12? God has both gifted you and placed you exactly where he wants you. You have a vital role to play on your team, in your church, and for Christ's kingdom.

The best teams recognize and appreciate the diversity of gifts on the team and employ them well. In my experience, teams that function well enjoy flexibility and freedom for individual team members under a broad umbrella of strategic agreement. Theology, methodology, and goals should be aligned. Everyone should understand and actively participate in the broader objectives and know the specific action steps driving their daily activities. In this way, team members live their lives with direction and purpose, knowing they can endure challenges because they are following God's will and in step with their co-laborers.

5. National Partners: Value local believers and work toward local ownership of the missionary task.

Local ownership of the core missionary tasks of evangelism, discipleship, church-planting, and leadership development should be a goal of every missionary team. Local churches send missionaries to cross linguistic, cultural, and geographic obstacles to preach the gospel and make faithful worshipers of the Lord Jesus. Therefore, the missionary team is a temporary reality that enables, equips, and serves local believers and churches so they can finish the task of reaching their communities and other unreached peoples.

To that end, relationships and partnerships with national Christians should be a top priority. This may mean sharing the gospel and seeing the first converts in some locations. In other places, this will mean assessing the strength and needs of local churches and humbly submitting to local pastors and institutions.

Teams that ignore or are apathetic toward national partners will find long-term success in ministry elusive. On the other hand, those teams who develop healthy attitudes and cultural understanding can leverage healthy relationships for kingdom-building purposes. Remember, you are not the ultimate key to reaching the people God loves. If multitudes of the lost in this generation and into the future will hear the gospel, it will be because of the faithful and voluntary commitment of local men and women who catch the vision and join God in his mission to their own people.

BEFORE YOU GO

AN EXTENDED FAMILY

A few months ago, our family enjoyed a visit from Aunt Tasha. Not too long after that, Uncle Joey and Aunt Christy came and stayed for a few days. My daughter recently graduated from high school, and she got messages from other aunts and uncles all around the world. The "family" members I am referring to won't make it on my official family tree of blood relatives. But many of them are as close to Amy, me, and our kids as our biological family.

Though I admitted above that I was initially uncomfortable with my first Thanksgiving in Zambia, later years would find us eager to travel to be with these dear friends for various holidays and gatherings. We came to depend on and love them because we did hard things together. We laughed hard, cried harder (I might be shedding a tear now as I write this), and loved one another through it all. In the years when I was far from my mother's kitchen, the Lord was kind to give us more than friends, more than a mentor, and even more than a team. He gave us a diverse family of missionary and national co-laborers, just as he promised in Mark 10:29–30. It is written:

> "Truly I tell you," Jesus said, "there is no one who has left house or brothers or sisters or mother or father or children or fields for my sake and for the sake of the gospel, who will not receive a hundred times more, now at this time—houses, brothers and sisters, mothers and children, and fields, with persecutions—and eternal life in the age to come."

DISCUSS AND REFLECT

1. What are five questions you would ask a potential team leader as you consider joining a team?

2. What specific spiritual gifts and skills do you possess that would complement a missionary team? Are you being faithful to use them in the context of your local church now?

3. How can you grow in building healthy relationships, specifically around resolving conflict?

4. How can you begin today to build cross-cultural relationships where you live?

CHAPTER 6

Prayer and Evangelism

Joe Allen III

From the General Editor

I (JOSH) AM thrilled to commend this chapter on evangelism and prayer by my good friend Joe Allen. I love this man and have seen him walk with the Lord for years. Our families have been friends for years, and we even lived in the same apartment complex overseas for a while. I have watched him cry as I frequently beat him at Ping-Pong between doctoral seminars. (He may dispute that claim.) More importantly, I have seen him labor in prayer over lost Muslims whom he longs to see worship the Lord Jesus. If you want to see Joe get excited, ask him a story about taking the good news into the villages of South Asia where he lived for fourteen years.

Joe is a master storyteller, and you will enjoy learning from him. Joe and his family lived where they were not always welcome. His life and safety were frequently in danger as he boldly proclaimed Jesus and trained national pastors to do the same. He models many things this book encourages, such as learning the local language, abiding in Christ, and leading your family well.

BEFORE YOU GO

Joe and his family served in two different countries in South Asia before he returned to the States to teach at Midwestern Seminary. I know that, rather than writing a chapter on this, he would prefer to take you into a village to speak face-to-face with some of the world's most unreached people. He believes and lives what he has written below about the necessity of prayer and the essential link between prayer and evangelism. Before you go, I trust that you already share the gospel with those around you and regularly pray for the lost. I trust Joe's chapter will provide practical strategies for prayer that will keep your heart and ministry aligned with the Lord's will for those he sends.

MIKE ON A BIKE

When I was a seminary student, I met a man named Mike at church. Everyone affectionately called him "Mike on a Bike" because of his love for cycling. His wise and gentle demeanor led me to ask if he would mentor me. He graciously agreed, so every Sunday, we would meet for Bible study and prayer, and then we would go to the local jail and share the gospel with the inmates. At the jail, we focused our attention on inmates isolated from the general population because of the high-profile nature of their crimes, misbehavior, or mental illness. On any given night, we would talk to murderers, drug dealers, or sexual predators.

Malcolm Gladwell argues that a person needs ten thousand hours of practice to gain an elite level of mastery,[14] but too many people give up on evangelism after just a few tries. I gained so much experience sharing the gospel during those years as I engaged with my captive audience. Just like a baseball player needs lots of at-bats to learn how to hit curveballs, sliders, and change-ups, there's no better way to learn evangelism than just doing it over and over!

One Sunday afternoon, while making his rounds, Mike stopped at the cell of a young man named Jeremy Zizloski. Jeremy had asked to speak with a chaplain, but the time for visitation was almost over. Before he left, Mike promised to return next week to speak with Jeremy.

That evening, at our church's prayer service, Mike sensed the Spirit compelling him to return to the jail and visit Jeremy. So, abruptly and uncharacteristically, Mike stood up and walked out of the service. He drove to the jail and got permission to visit Jeremy. For about forty-five minutes, Mike explained that Jesus died on the cross for Jeremy's sins and rose from the dead. Mike pled with him, and that night, Jeremy made the eternity-altering decision to place his faith in the Lord Jesus.

PRAYER AND EVANGELISM REINFORCE ONE ANOTHER

In this chapter, you might initially expect to find prayer paired with fasting or evangelism with discipleship. But in this chapter, I want to argue that prayer and evangelism go together like chocolate and peanut butter. The two practices mutually reinforce one another and enhance the other spiritual disciplines. The dynamic happens like this: the more you pray, the more you attune your heart to God's heart, and specifically, God's heart for the lost. The more you seek to evangelize, the more you sense your need for the Holy Spirit's divine enablement and long for his intervention.

BEFORE YOU GO

Prayer should lead to gospel proclamation, and gospel proclamation should intensify your prayers.

The irony is that prayer is often a solitary activity that appeals to introverts, while evangelism is a social activity that appeals to extroverts. Regardless of your personality, maintaining a close interrelationship between prayer and evangelism will push you out of your comfort zone and force you to grow. When you join prayer and evangelism, watch out! Something special is about to happen.

Jesus links prayer and evangelism in Luke 10:2 when he says, "The harvest is abundant, but the workers are few. Therefore, pray to the Lord of the harvest to send out workers into his harvest." Jesus instructs his disciples to pray for harvesters and then, in a surprising twist, he sends them to be the answer to their own prayers! The same thing might happen to you, so when you pray, be ready to obey.

A verse that I find myself returning to time and again when I think about prayer and evangelism is Romans 10:1. Here, we get a glimpse of Paul's heart, which proves instructive for us. He writes: "my heart's desire and prayer to God concerning them is for their salvation." As we consider the importance of prayer and evangelism in the life of a missionary, let me make three observations about this verse.

First, Paul *cared deeply*. His desire was not a shallow, fleeting desire, but a core longing that sprang from the center of his being. If you do not feel deep compassion for the lost, go back and review the gospel. Consider afresh the glory of the One who calls you into fellowship with him. Meditate on the majesty of God as revealed in Scripture. Think about the sacrifice of Jesus and the depth of the love that bought your salvation. Contemplate the joys of heaven and the horrors of hell until your heart is stirred for others to know the gospel. Feed your godly desires so you can say with Paul, "My heart's desire and prayer to God concerning them is for their salvation."

Second, Paul *prayed fervently*. The people of Israel had rejected Jesus as their Messiah, but Paul remained hopeful that they might be saved. Paul did not give up on them, and he did not leave his heart's desire unexpressed; he acted. That action first took the form of prayer. We must do the same. Do not bottle up your desire; let it bubble up and overflow in prayer. Give expression to your desire through intercession.

Third, Paul *prayed specifically*. He did not pray ambiguous prayers for some amorphous spiritual blessing. Instead, he prayed for their salvation. Elsewhere, Paul prayed for boldness (Eph. 6:18–20), for opportunity (Col. 4:2–4), and that the Word of the Lord would spread rapidly and be glorified (2 Thess. 3:1). A couple of years ago, I realized that if I only make vague or general requests with lots of qualifications and caveats, then I would never be able to tell if God had answered. So let me encourage you to pray such focused prayers for the salvation of souls so that you can recognize God's answers and rejoice.

THE BURDEN OF PRAYER AND EVANGELISM

If you're reading this book, you probably affirm the importance of prayer and evangelism. Still, these disciplines are two of the most difficult, uncomfortable, and guilt-inducing for most Christians. A depressing cloud of shame threatens to suffocate many of us for our failures in these areas. We already know we don't pray enough and don't evangelize enough. Plus, you probably feel a special urgency to grow in prayer and evangelism if you're preparing to become a missionary. Yet, even missionaries willing to make great personal sacrifices to bring the gospel across boundaries often find themselves faltering in their prayer life and evangelistic efforts.

When we receive training in prayer or evangelism, we often find ourselves looking to a prayer prodigy or evangelism expert. Unfortunately, those on the platform are either unusually contemplative or unusually outgoing. Their peculiar temperaments would have led them to become hermits or salesmen had they not gone into Christian ministry. While expertise is obviously good, the problem is that regular Christians can leave such trainings feeling defeated and stuck, rather than inspired and equipped. So, what should sincere believers do to overcome the intellectual, emotional, and practical hurdles to prayer and evangelism? How can we integrate these important activities into our daily lives in a God-glorifying, sustainable, yet non-legalistic way? Let me give you six pieces of advice for ordinary Christian evangelism and prayer.

Apply the Gospel to Prayer and Evangelism

First, we must fundamentally reorient our thoughts and feelings about prayer and evangelism. Instead of viewing prayer and evangelism as items on a checklist or obligations to appease an unsmiling God, we must apply the gospel to our prayer life and evangelistic efforts. But, you might ask, "What does that mean?"

I am glad you asked. The gospel shows us that, because of Jesus, God is already smiling at us. When viewed through a gospel lens, we see prayer as a marvelous and indispensable means of fellowship with this God who has willingly adopted us into his family. With a focus on our reception of this good news, the gospel helps us see evangelism as the verbal overflow of our own experience of God's goodness to us. Only the gospel can shift these disciplines from drudgery to delight.

Gospel-Centered Prayer and Evangelism

Second, gospel-centered prayer and evangelism foster intimacy with God in a way that few other activities do. When you delve deeper into the gospel, you become aware of your desperation for God and the cost of your salvation. Confronted by God's holiness and your sinfulness, you begin to glimpse the depth of God's love displayed in the crucifixion of Jesus. As you grasp the good news of the gospel for yourself, you will naturally begin to see the importance of declaring this message to others. Evangelism then becomes an awe-filled response to the grace you've received. Powered by the gospel, prayer and evangelism become joyful practices that nurture intimacy with God and fruitfulness for God.

As a way to guide some of your prayer and presentation, consider the following conveniently alliterated summary of the gospel's effects. The gospel begins with God's righteous initiative, sending his eternal Son to assume humanity, live a perfect life, die a substitutionary death, and rise triumphant over sin, death, and Satan (1 Cor. 15:1–5). Through this gospel, our triune God rescues us (Col. 1:13), regenerates us (Titus 3:5), redeems us (Eph. 1:7), reconciles us (Col. 1:22), ransoms us (Matt. 20:28), raises us (Eph. 2:6), restores us (Ezek. 36:36; 1 Pet. 5:10), releases us from sin (Rom. 6:18), recreates us (2 Cor. 4:6; 5:17), and resurrects us (Rom. 6:5).

The gospel is simply the good news that all of this is true because God has initiated our rescue for his glory. He pours out his love into our hearts, using his people and his Word to deliver the message, and we respond in personal faith in his promises and provision. Having experienced God's love, we can love others. Therefore, two of the most practical ways to love your neighbor are (1) to pray for your neighbor's salvation and (2) to tell your neighbor the message of salvation.

Internalize the Gospel, Vocalize the Gospel

Third, the gospel is good news because it is the message of God's great love. Nowhere is God's love more vividly on display than at the cross: "God demonstrates His own love toward us, in that while we were still sinners, Christ died for us" (Rom. 5:8 NASB). Intentionally internalize this reality. Preach it to your heart, dwell on it, study it, write poems about it, paint pictures of it, meditate on it, memorize Scriptures about it, discuss it with others, and sing about it! Be so absorbed in it that it transforms your heart and mind and changes the way you live and speak. Christians of old talked about "feasting on the gospel," by which they meant enjoying the banquet of blessings secured by Jesus. By savoring the gospel, Jesus grows precious to us.

The most effective evangelists are the ones who have first evangelized their own hearts, because you can't give what you don't have. Embrace God's grace for yourself so you can be a channel of grace to others. Jesus says, "the mouth speaks from the overflow of the heart" (Matt. 12:34), so the more the gospel blows your mind and transforms your heart, the more your mouth will utter prayers to God and the gospel to others. The key to *vocalizing* the gospel is first *internalizing* the gospel.

Pray for Boldness in Evangelism

Fourth, treasuring Christ does not completely remove fear and trepidation in evangelism. Timothy Beougher, professor of evangelism at The Southern Baptist Theological Seminary, tells a story about the first time he met Billy Graham. He writes:

> I had the privilege of spending an hour with him as we walked through the museum at the Billy Graham Center on Wheaton's campus. I had envisioned this day for some time and had a long list of questions about evangelism I wanted to ask him. But when I met him, my mind went blank. I blurted out the only question that came to my mind: "Mr. Graham, do you ever feel nervous when you are witnessing to someone one-on-one?" He looked at me like that was the stupidest question he had ever heard, but when he saw it was a serious question, he replied, "Of course! Who doesn't? In fact, if I didn't feel a bit nervous, I would assume I was witnessing in my own strength. God allows us to feel a bit nervous, so we will trust in him and his power."[15]

But it is not just Billy Graham that needs to overcome fear. Even the apostle Paul asked for boldness in evangelism. He writes: "pray in my behalf, that speech may be given to me in the opening of my mouth, to make known with boldness the mystery of the gospel" (Eph. 6:19 NASB). Take heart—if evangelism causes you to fear, you are in good company.

Do Not Seek a Technique

Fifth, we would love to find a silver bullet or a one-size-fits-all approach to evangelism, but Eckhard Schnabel reminds us: "In mission and evangelism the search for a method that will guarantee success in our attempt to convince listeners of the truth of the gospel of Jesus Christ is misguided."[16] If there is no guaranteed key to success, wouldn't it at least be nice to find a way to minimize the awkwardness of evangelism? Sure, but we can't let awkwardness deter us. J. I. Packer urges: "If (as is usual) it is the fear of being thought odd and ridiculous, or losing popularity in certain circles, that holds us back, we need to ask ourselves in the presence of God: Ought these things to stop us loving our neighbor? . . . We need to press on our conscience this question: Which matters more—our reputation or their salvation?"[17]

Have you ever felt uncomfortable trying to bring up the gospel in conversation? That's not unusual. Getting started is usually the hardest part. I've been greatly encouraged by Brian Zunigha, who says, "Awkward conversations change lives."[18] Embrace the awkwardness. Don't let the fear of social discomfort keep you from speaking up for Jesus. Let love overcome your natural aversion to awkward conversations.

Prayer and Evangelism Are Relational Activities

And finally, sixth, for Christians, prayer is not about rules, rote recitation, or ritual. Prayer is about a *relationship*—communion with our heavenly Father through the Son and by the

Spirit. If prayer was primarily about performing, we would need to concern ourselves with external forms. Should I stand, kneel, or lay down? Should I raise my hands with palms up, palms out, or should I fold my hands? Should I bow my head and close my eyes or look up into heaven? The Bible mentions a wide variety of prayer postures, and our physical posture can undoubtedly affect our attitude, but we must emphasize the posture of our heart. If prayer is about spending time with God, perhaps the best way to conceptualize prayer is like a child walking hand-in-hand with his father or simply crawling up in his father's lap.

Evangelism is also deeply relational. We must never treat those far from God as "targets." We must avoid the mindset of a door-to-door salesperson. Instead, we must view other people as created in the image of God with inestimable value, and love them enough to speak with frankness and compassion. Embracing the relational nature of evangelism, some people have adopted "friendship evangelism," an approach that builds relationships with people over the course of months or years before getting to the gospel. Instead of friendship evangelism, consider "friendly evangelism." Friendly evangelism is an approach that seeks to establish sincere rapport with the other person but does not hesitate to bring up the gospel right away. Friendly evangelism keeps the relationship front and center without minimizing the urgency and importance of speaking the gospel from the very beginning.

BEFORE YOU GO

A FEW PRACTICAL POINTERS

Here are half a dozen practical ideas to help you integrate rhythms of prayer and evangelism into your daily life. These suggestions will help you move from theory to practice.

1. Use your calendar. Set recurring reminders to pray and schedule regular times for outreach. If you only "catch as catch can," you will find that other activities squeeze out your priorities.

2. Find a partner. The Bible doesn't explain the reasons Jesus sent out his disciples two-by-two, but a moment's reflection reveals the wisdom of this approach. A partner will help you avoid discouragement, provide fellowship and accountability, protect against temptations, pick up the conversation when you get stuck, and support you with prayer.

3. Journal your prayers. If you find your mind wandering in prayer, pray out loud or write out your prayers. Journaling has the benefit of not only focusing your thoughts and fighting against distraction, but you will also have a record of your requests and the ways God answers them.

4. Riff on a passage of Scripture. Extemporaneous prayer is a valid and sweet way to pour out your heart to God, but you can significantly enrich your communication with God by using a passage of Scripture as a springboard for your prayers. Personalize the words of the Bible. Read a passage of Scripture and pray it back to God, asking him to help you understand his will, believe his promises, and apply his commands.

5. Memorize a few opening questions. Often, the most challenging part of evangelism is getting started. Talking about the gospel is usually pretty natural once the conversation moves in a spiritual direction. Two of my favorite lines are, "Do you have any spiritual beliefs?" and "What do you think is the biggest problem in the world?"[19] Most people enjoy talking about themselves, and if you show genuine curiosity and care for the other person, they will usually be happy to talk about their beliefs.

6. Monitor your love. Regarding both prayer and evangelism, ask yourself if love is the driving force. If not, you "have become a noisy gong or a clanging cymbal" (1 Cor. 13:1 NASB). The moment you slip into a performance mindset, you become self-absorbed. Then fear, anxiety, and burdens will choke out your love. Instead, you must rekindle your love for God and others by total immersion in the gospel.

BEFORE YOU GO

THE POWER OF PRAYER

The early American pastor Lemuel Haynes asked, "Can there be a more delightful employment, this side of heaven, than to send the blessed news of salvation to a perishing world?"[20] Mike knew this joy. A few days after Mike led Jeremy to the Lord, he was at home flipping through the newspaper. A name in the obituary section caught his attention: Zizloski. The obituary explained that Jeremy had experienced an epileptic seizure in his cell. When he fell, he hit his head on a concrete ledge and died immediately. Mike shuddered to think how he would have felt had he not made that extra effort to bring the gospel to Jeremy, but his grief was mixed with joy because he knew the young man was now with the Lord.

Mike thought he might be able to track down Jeremy's family because Zizloski was such an unusual last name. After a little searching, Mike found a single listing for Zizloski in his area. So he made the call and found himself talking to Jeremy's grandparents.

When Mike recounted the story of their grandson's conversion, there was a long pause on the phone followed by weeping. Between sobs, Jeremy's grandparents related how they had been praying for Jeremy's salvation for twenty years. They told Mike how Jeremy would not listen to them talk about the gospel. For years, he had steadfastly rejected the Lord Jesus. They thought Jeremy was hardened to the gospel, but they continued praying.

Hearing Mike's story filled them with unspeakable joy. They tried to find words to thank Mike for his sensitivity to the Spirit and his faithfulness in sharing the gospel. They thanked him for seeking them out and calling to tell them the story. They marveled and praised God for answering their prayers—two long decades of prayers.

God has chosen to work through prayer and evangelism. He works through believers to accomplish his mission on earth. As you prepare to become a missionary, elevate your vision of God as your heavenly Father who lovingly rules over the universe. Clarify your perception of Jesus as the divine-human Savior who suffered the ultimate humiliation and now enjoys the ultimate exaltation. Deepen your dependence on the Holy Spirit, who advocates for you and accomplishes God's will through you. Saturate yourself in the gospel until you appreciate what God has done for you and in you. Let the gospel motivate you to pray and evangelize, and then watch as God works through you.

PRAYER

The following prayer is from the Puritan pastor Joseph Alleine:

> *For those who do not know you yet, Lord, grab on to them now, and do your work. Take them by the heart, overcome them, and persuade them, until they say, "You have won. You are stronger than I." Lord, did you not make me a fisher of men? I have worked all this time and caught nothing. Have I spent my strength for nothing? I will cast my net one more time. Lord Jesus, stand on the shore and show me how and where to spread my net. Give me the words to enclose the souls I seek, that they will have no way out. Now, Lord, for a multitude of souls.*

BEFORE YOU GO

Now for a full portion. Lord God, remember me, I pray, and strengthen me, O God. Amen.[21]

DISCUSS AND REFLECT

1. How do you need the gospel to reorient your thinking about prayer and evangelism?

2. Does your temperament gravitate more toward prayer or evangelism?

3. Who could you team up with for prayer and evangelism?

4. Who can you recruit to pray that you will have boldness?

CHAPTER 7

Going Single

Matt Rhodes

From the General Editor

A COUPLE OF years ago I (Matt) read a book titled *No Shortcut to Success*, written by Matt Rhodes. In the book, Matt challenged missionaries to push for deep language acquisition, robust engagement with culture, and solid theological training and preparation. Given some of the trends in missiology that call such building blocks into question in the name of urgency, Rhodes' perspective was a breath of fresh air.

I had the opportunity to meet Matt and his wife in 2022. In hearing their story, I was immediately even more impressed than when he was just an author of a book I appreciated. While Matt and I do not have a long history together, I find in him a kindred spirit and one whose example and advice are worth following.

Part of Matt's story is that he spent a significant part of his life as a single man serving on the mission field. Single missionaries make up a large percentage of the missionary force, and it is important to consider how this demographic reality plays into presenting both unique opportunities and particular struggles. In the chapter that follows, Matt provides sage advice for singles who are looking to serve Jesus with all that they are wherever and with whomever the Lord places them.

Even if you are married, it is likely that you will have single teammates. Before you go, this chapter will be edifying to all readers as it provides insight into what it looks like to team and work together despite different life circumstances.

ME, GOD, AND MY DONKEY

Like an anxious, recurring dream, I often found myself replaying a future scene in my imagination during the low points of my first years on the mission field. In it, I would stand before the judgment seat, and Jesus would say, "Well done, good and faithful servant!" (Matt. 25:23).

Then, before letting me in through the pearly gates, he would pause uncomfortably and say, "Just so you know, I never understood what you were doing alone in Africa all those years. I'd really hoped you would settle down and get married." Then, in this imaginary future scene, he would shrug and gesture me through the gates saying, "Well, anyway, welcome home."

As you can tell, I struggle with an overactive imagination. I also struggled at some low points with my singleness. I'd passed up opportunities to pursue strong Christian girls because they weren't headed for missions work. And after a few years of hoping I would meet someone on the field, the missed opportunities started to weigh on me.

But those years had high points too. There were times when I felt supremely confident in my singleness. On one such occasion, I remember traveling by donkey across a bleak, war-torn stretch of desert with three men from an unreached Muslim tribe. The hot North African sun was burning my feet lobster-red through the holes in my sandals, and I was thinking, *I could spend the rest of my life like this.*

The whole scene felt so right—so faithful, so Book-of-Acts-like, so extreme. I didn't need to marry. I didn't need anything at all. It would be me, God, and the donkey I was riding on, leading a small unreached country to Christ. Did I mention my overactive imagination?

The confusing thing was that, despite those high points where God felt so close, I couldn't get rid of the low points. The intense loneliness. The despair. The second-guessing. What made it worse was that I felt I was failing Jesus at these low points by not drawing total satisfaction from him. People I admired urged me to draw closer to Jesus as if to suggest that the joyful intensity of those high points wouldn't be so elusive if I leaned more consistently on him.

Lord, why am I so faithless? I wondered, *Why can't I just be satisfied with you?*

A BIBLICAL VIEW OF SINGLENESS

In retrospect, neither I nor the well-meaning people advising me understood what the Scriptures say about singleness. Few Christians do. A friend of mine, in a bitter moment, once declared that the gift of singleness was the white-elephant gift of the Holy Spirit. While he was exaggerating for effect, he accurately voiced the conflict many Christians feel about singleness. On the one hand, we know it's a gift. On the other hand, we're not sure we want it!

Our churches and missions communities feed this sense of conflicted identity. Singles are encouraged—as I was—that if they draw close enough to Jesus, they'll be perfectly content. But at the same time, the structures of church life tend to treat singles as incomplete people, making them feel like uncomfortable outsiders. There's no shortage of sermons on marriage, marriage retreats, and couples' small groups. Singles groups and events are few and far between, and singles instinctively know they need to justify attending them by saying things like: "I started going to our church's singles group, and it's not a meat market at all!" Singles regularly hear their status mourned: "We can't believe he's still single! He's such a great guy," or ominously fretted about: "If he wants to get married someday, he'll have to learn to be more of a team player."

Unfortunately, on some teams, singles are thought to have less wisdom and life experience than their married teammates. This can translate into having less of a voice in making strategic team decisions. Being less limited by family responsibilities, singles can be treated as if they have unlimited capacity. The workload can then be disproportionately assigned to singles, assuming they have more time and energy to spare. In extreme cases, teams of married couples can come to view singles more as babysitters than as partners in ministry.

The underlying message is that singleness is a sort of larval stage of humanity and ministry capacity. Someday, when you get married, you'll mature into a beautiful butterfly.

But none of this is scriptural. The apostle Paul didn't see singles as unfortunate failures-to-launch. To Paul, singleness was a mark of *self-control and maturity*. He writes: "I say to the unmarried and to the widows: It is good for them if they remain as I am. But if they do not have self-control, they should marry, since it is better to marry than to burn with desire" (1 Cor. 7:8–9).

His view is different enough that it almost leaves you wondering if he would ask married people—rather than singles—to justify their status: *Wow, you sure got married young. Did you really have so little self-control?* Only that's not where he goes. Instead of criticizing either singles or marrieds, Paul simply says, "But each has his own gift from God, one person has this gift, another has that" (v. 7).

He explains that each of us can find our gifting by pursuing whichever life situations—married or single, slave or free (vv. 21–24)—best allow us to pursue God with undistracted focus. If desire and loneliness distract us from pursuing God, we should seek to marry. But marriage, which is a good gift from God, comes with some additional concerns and responsibilities. Paul writes later in this chapter: "The unmarried man is concerned about the things of the Lord—how he may please the Lord. But the married man is concerned about the things of the world—how he may please his wife—and his interests are divided" (vv. 32b–34a).

In other words, the complexity marriage adds to life is *inherently* distracting, so if we can pursue God undistracted as singles, we should do so. But, regardless of our particular ministry shape and the circumstances in which we find ourselves, we should not miss that Paul refers to both these stations—married or single—as gifts.

BEFORE YOU GO

PRACTICAL TAKEAWAYS IF YOU ARE NOT GIFTED FOR SINGLENESS

So how do we know which gift is for us? All of us are born single, but that doesn't mean all of us are gifted to serve God well by remaining that way. Singles who have significant struggles with desire or loneliness shouldn't assume that their struggles are evidence that they are failing to find satisfaction in Jesus alone. Of course, you should draw as close to Jesus as you can! But there may be types of loneliness given to us that will not be fulfilled merely by conjuring up more faith. Even before the fall, it was "not good" for Adam to be alone (Gen. 2:18). Single missionaries who have found healthy sustenance in Jesus's presence alone may be gifted in ways you are not. As spiritual as it may sound to say, "I've chosen to find satisfaction in God rather than in marriage," this can be an *unspiritual* decision if it involves choosing a path God clearly hasn't ordained. Instead, if singleness causes significant distress in your walk with God, you should pursue marriage without shame. Paul urges his readers to do precisely this, suggesting that "it is better to marry than to burn with desire" (1 Cor. 7:9).

Pursuing marriage is an active process. I've seen missionaries slowly consumed by loneliness and grief on remote fields who remained convinced that if God wanted them to marry, he would bring a spouse to them. But we don't approach any other life decision that way. If you need a job, you look for a job. You might even move to a city that has more jobs. You'd probably feel it was lazy to wait around for a job to come to you. Finding a good spouse is far more important than finding a job, so you may need to exercise some diligence and intentionality. Abraham knew God wanted to give him descendants through Isaac, but he didn't just wait for a wife for Isaac to show up. He sent a treasure-laden caravan halfway across the known world to find Rebekah.

Here, I'll let you in on an open secret of mission field life. For as long as anyone can remember, single women have outnumbered single men on the mission field by a significant margin. For example, a single guy friend of mine was on a team with a couple who served as the team leaders for a team composed of eleven single women.

Now, before you take my comments above as a new dating strategy, I'll remind you that, of course, numerical odds don't guarantee you'll find a suitable spouse on the mission field. No one can promise that, on or off the field. And if you're the only guy on a field with three single women, that still isn't a large pool to choose from—and they might not choose you! So, if you don't sense you can pursue God undistracted as a single, you should avoid long-term placements where you have little chance to meet a partner.

This is not to say that you should avoid going when or where the Lord and your church send you. Instead, understanding your giftedness to serve well in the ministry situations you are considering is a part of discerning where God is sending you. If singleness is a significant struggle for you and you still believe you are called to go, think with your church about targeting fields where you can serve with a significant community of singles. Cairo or Istanbul is better than the remote mountains of northern Pakistan! You might even plan to make your budget include room for dating and—if you meet someone with real potential—for traveling.

And let me give you permission to embrace some contemporary means of connecting with like-minded people on the field.

Don't discount the potential of connecting with single women who are like-minded about missions work via Christian online dating venues or at missionary conferences. Just make sure to have the support of your sending church. Find ways to work under leaders who support you as you do so, knowing that this will involve some traveling outside of your place of service if the relationship gains momentum. You won't be able to make relationship decisions wisely without getting to know someone well and spending real time with her.

I want to clarify here that I am not assuming you to be "desperate" or "uncontrolled" if you find yourself longing for marriage. I'm also not telling you to fixate on your need for a spouse to the exclusion of everything else. Instead, I'm telling you to let it have significant space in your life, since it's a significant consideration, and to be ready to let your search for a spouse affect your ministry. After all, if you get married, your marriage will undoubtedly affect your ministry. And it's bigger than your ministry. Your ministry may change over the coming years—fields can close or health problems may force you to return home, but marriage is a lifelong commitment!

Still, field-bound singles tend to fight this. I've heard singles describe their road to the field as a "conveyor belt" they can't get off of and tell me: "I can't tell my supporters I'm changing direction to find a *girl*!" Not long ago, a single confided: "I don't know how I'm going to survive on the field alone, but I can't tell my church that. They wouldn't understand. So, I tell them I'm fine." Doubtless, these individuals' sending churches admire their determination. But I've seen how these cases play out. Singles who begin this way will either meet and marry someone on the field, or else at some point in their thirties, they'll predictably feel called back home. Though they'll still often feel the need to offer something other than their singleness as a reason for coming off the field.

The odd thing is, few of us would let the feeling of being on an unstoppable conveyor belt drive us into marriage—shouldn't we be equally slow to let that feeling drive us to places where we have few chances to marry? Singles who feel this way need to tell their sending churches the truth. Tell them going it alone may seem heroic, but harder roads aren't always better roads. Sometimes it's braver to be up-front about our needs. Ask your sending church to read this chapter, if it helps. They may be more gracious than you imagine.

Be honest with yourself about how other people's opinions influence you. We all have people whose approval we value intensely. However, be careful how much you value people's opinions who will think more of you if you go overseas. However well-motivated these people may be, if you go overseas, you will need to know you went to please God, not to please them.

And for Paul, the decision of whether to marry or to stay single is primarily about seeking God. Singles are often led to hope that if they handle singleness well, God will bless them with a good marriage, and particularly, single men are led to hope that if they abstain from premarital sex, God will give them great sex when they do marry. Now God may do this, but he never promises it. Instead, he promises us eternal life with him. Singles, if Christ's promises are true, then the best marriage you could find won't hold a candle to the reward God has prepared for you. Honor God in your singleness for *his* sake and for the prize *he* promises.

BEFORE YOU GO

PRACTICAL TAKEAWAYS IF YOU ARE GIFTED FOR SINGLENESS

And for those gifted as singles, I want to explain why Paul sees your gift as preferable to marriage. Paul never suggests we pursue singleness for its own sake, and he never reverses God's pronouncement in the garden that it isn't good for a man to be alone. Instead, he gives us two reasons to pursue singleness.

First, marriage produces divided and distracted energies and attention in our fallen world. Paul writes: "But such people will have trouble in this life" (1 Cor. 7:28), meaning that they have taken on responsibilities that will come with relational frustrations, trouble, and concerns that will be apportioned differently for those not married. While marriage is intended to celebrate union and mutual love, marriage is also prone to fall apart in shockingly destructive ways. Rather than missionaries being immune to marital strife and stress, the pressures of the mission field can exacerbate some of these tensions for two people who are still in the process of sanctification.

Second, we must recognize the urgency of the hour. Paul would have gifted singles avoid even the best of marriages because, as he says, the "time is limited" and "this world in its current form is passing away" (vv. 29, 31). Yet, Paul sees a chance for gifted singles to invest in a world that will last. Singles who exhibit the "self-control" (v. 9) that Paul identifies as a marker of the gift of singleness can remain clear-sighted enough to see what an urgent need and incredible opportunity it is to serve King Jesus single-mindedly while his return tarries.

Notice that Paul doesn't say gifted singles will always find singleness easy to bear. He simply says singleness will be a better situation for them than marriage. Let's be clear: there's no *easy* way out of it for anyone. Singles struggle with loneliness, and married people have marriage problems.

Thankfully, singles and married people can still live fulfilling lives, especially if both are ready to reach out for whatever help they need. But this may take some real effort! As a gifted single, you can minister with endurance and flexibility married people can't. Don't be surprised then if, like a long-distance runner, you sometimes require special nourishment. Be diligent to put in place the emotional disciplines, spiritual practices, and social networks your situation requires as you pursue biblical faithfulness and healthy support for your race.

WHERE MY JOURNEY LED

My single years became more fulfilling as I established a wide network of friendships and learned ways to handle my emotional needs. While single on the field, I'd melt down completely once or twice a week. Not outwardly—most of the time, no one noticed. But inwardly, I'd find myself in really despairing places, thinking, *I just don't have what it takes. I hate being on the field. I hate being alone. I can't do this anymore. I can't. I can't. I can't.* This would last thirty minutes to an hour, then I'd feel buoyant again. Once I realized this was just a strange emotional rhythm that would come and go, I could handle the downswings better. Over time I learned to cultivate more of an eternal mindset—to remember that married or single, what I'm living for is the next life, and this whole life is only a practice run. In fact, my struggles with singleness played an indispensable role in helping me remember and more deeply understand that.

It took me years to understand Scripture's teaching about singleness and to discern my gifting. In the end, I had what I would describe as strategic and temporary gifting for singleness. I was happy overall, but the desire to marry persisted, and the sharp downswings never disappeared. These tendencies weren't disabling, but they were strong enough to indicate that, over the long term, I could better pursue God in a good marriage rather than single.

I learned that the me-and-God-and-my-donkey intensity that had convinced me of my ability to stay single was a personality trait, not a spiritual strength. It could lead me toward God and bring me to give up my career and homeland for Christ. But it could also cause me to ignore my own God-given needs and personal weaknesses. And it could cause me to do the same for others around me in ways that resulted in me becoming demanding and judgmental. And slowly, I learned how to replace my intensity in real spiritual wisdom.

And that's where I was for years. I pursued marriage actively. I utilized reputable online dating sites. I gave up my desire for marriage. Yet, my desire for marriage came back. So I tried to give up the desire for marriage again. And again. And nothing changed.

After almost nine years on the field, I did get married. I won't say much about that here, not because Kim isn't amazing—she is!—but because my story didn't have to end that way. More to the point, I realize *your* story may not end that way. And ultimately, neither singleness nor marriage is the end of anyone's story.

Kim and I are no longer single, but one day, when "death do us part," either Kim or I will be single again. But, even that will not be the end of the story. Death will not only separate us but will unite us once again in resurrection, not in marriage, as we know it here on earth, but in something closer and indescribably better. And Christ will come to claim his bride, and the marriage we've been waiting for—the one that's too beautiful and amazing for even my overactive imagination to conceive of—will take place. And we'll finally be freed for real from this larval stage and unfold our wings, and the practice run will be over, and our real life will have begun. We will no longer be single or married, but we will all be joined with the rest of the saints in union with Christ.

DISCUSS AND REFLECT

1. Have you seen singleness as an incomplete or "larval" stage? What is it, scripturally, that makes singleness or marriage advantageous?

2. What are some indicators that might guide you to pursue either singleness or marriage? It took the author years to discern his gifting. Do you need time to discern your path?

3. If you suspect you aren't gifted for singleness and are considering the mission field, what steps can you take to find a healthy field environment? Will your desire to marry influence your decision to go, your field destination, or the timing of your departure?

4. If you sense you might be gifted as a single, what emotional disciplines, spiritual practices, and social networks can you put in place to make the most of your singleness?

CHAPTER 8

Family and Mission

Brian Harrell

From the General Editor

WHAT IF FOLLOWING God's call on your life means raising your children in rural Africa? Is it possible to not only survive but thrive? Will your kids hate you if they miss out on all the opportunities in America? These are possibly the types of questions some of you may be considering as you prepare to go.

I (Josh) met Brian and his young family almost twenty years ago at a strategy training meeting in South Africa. I was blessed to see Brian and his wife, Becky, as they loved their children well and intentionally included them in their ministry. Amazingly, he has also taught his kids how to spearfish off the coast of Africa! Brian has the respect and admiration of his colleagues, the nationals to whom he ministers, and most importantly, his bride and children.

I encourage you to listen to his stories, words of wisdom, and encouragement on how to shepherd your family as you fulfill your mutual calling. It is a huge responsibility to jump on a plane with young children and take them far away from family and familiarity. You may be wondering how you will educate your children and what friendships will look like. Like any of us, Brian would admit he hasn't gotten it all right. Nonetheless, before you go, there are some essential things you can learn from him about being a father and husband.

Brian still lives along the coast of Africa, sharing the Good News. You will be blessed as he shares the biblical responsibility to abide in Christ as a family. I pray that you will recognize the tremendous privilege and blessing you will experience as a family on mission with God. I trust that by the end of this chapter, your faith will be increased, and the way you frame questions about family and mission will be different as well.

MISSIONARY KIDS

African land borders are always stressful to navigate, especially with four children in tow. You hope you catch the government officials on a good day as long lines form amidst an uneasy bustle of everyone trying to cross the border. However, I have always appreciated my competent and confident wife, who allows us to divide and conquer. I braved the chaos of temporary import permits, third-party car insurance, and customs as she huddled our little band together to fill out entry cards and have passports stamped. In haste, she scribbled on her own entry card that her occupation was "child." Next to her, our second son filled out his entry card for the first time. In the chaos of the customs office, my son reflected on his answer to the question of his occupation, and scribbled down the word *missionary*.

My wife and I had a good laugh as she recounted the story, and we were waved through the gate and went on our way. I was happy as I looked at the face of my contented son bouncing along behind me. But, at the same time, questions arose in my mind: Does he know what a missionary is? Did he write this to please his parents? My wife and I are missionaries; are our kids missionaries too?

When we first headed overseas, almost twenty years ago, someone asked us if we planned to take our one-year-old son with us to Africa. Perhaps you are there right now, wondering what raising a family and doing ministry on the field will look like for you. What follows are some words of advice that I hope will encourage you to trust that if God is trustworthy to provide for you, he is trustworthy to provide for your family.

THE RESPONSIBILITY TO LEAD OUR KIDS WELL

In Luke 6:39–40, Jesus tells a parable, saying, "Can the blind guide the blind? Won't they both fall into a pit? A disciple is not above his teacher, but everyone who is fully trained will be like his teacher." Jesus's teaching on discipleship is sobering for anyone seeking godliness. A disciple will become like the one who trains him. Furthermore, a teacher cannot impart that which he does not have.

As I headed to the mission field, I was reminded that my first disciples were my wife and one-year-old son. Indeed, as husbands, we are charged to lead, love, and cherish our wives as Christ does his bride, the church (Eph. 5:25). As fathers, we are the ones tasked with the responsibility to nurture our children in the discipline and instruction of the Lord (6:4). We cannot give what we are not. In fact, our families will take on many of the character traits and habits they learn from us. Brothers, that is a sobering thought, which makes me profoundly grateful for the lavish grace of God. Praise the Lord that we are instruments in the hand of the Master! We have a God-given responsibility to lead our families well as we live among the nations for the sake of the gospel. How, then, should we lead?

LEAD YOUR FAMILY IN LIFE AND MINISTRY WITH THE END IN MIND

Every believer longs to hear God speak these words from Matthew 25:21 at the end of their lives: "Well done, good and faithful servant! You were faithful over a few things; I will put you in charge of many things. Share the master's joy."

There are many ways to measure success in missions. Some prefer measuring breadth, others depth, and everyone claims they are after health. It is easy to set up our metric, which may lead us to measure ourselves and others in unhealthy ways. But, with God, there is one principle measurement for success: faithfulness.

As a missionary, you will regularly report your progress on language and cultural acquisition as well as the development and implementation of your strategy. The temptation is to compare, compete, and measure yourself by your productivity. But remember, there is One to whom you will give an account, and his measure is: "Have you been faithful?"

The same metric of faithfulness applies to your family life on the field. A faithful husband and father is far more than one who keeps himself from infidelity. A faithful husband remembers the vows he made on his wedding day to love and cherish. A faithful

FAMILY AND MISSION

father recognizes that his children are an inheritance (Ps. 127:3) to bring up in the discipline and instruction of the Lord (Eph. 6:4 ESV). Hear me on this, a faithful husband and father does not organize his life around safety, protection, comfort, or rights to a particular lifestyle. Instead, he holds all these things in submission to the pursuit of faithfulness to God.

Faithfulness is not a mundane characteristic; far from it. Faithfulness is our unwavering obedience to the Lord. It is our constant yes before the Lord, which springs from a heart that says, "Speak, LORD, for your servant hears" (1 Sam. 3:9 ESV). That is a radical statement that will take you to a place where only God's grace will sustain you. Faithfulness brings focus and clarity to your personal life, marriage, family life, and ministry. Faithfulness brings balance and rest as you seek to please the One who has called you.

At this point in the chapter, I have not said much that is new. However, the stress you are about to undergo as a disciple, husband, and father in a cross-cultural setting will make it imperative to be well-versed in these fundamental truths. I remember coming to the field and being incompetent in basic communication. I was more inefficient in my work than I could have imagined. My immediate support circle shrank dramatically as friends and family said goodbye. Waves of culture shock sent tremors through my family for some time. What was "normal" in my marriage and my family radically changed as we adapted to a new life. During all this time of testing, God showed me so much about myself. Faithfulness back "home" seemed so much easier. Yet, God was faithful both to convict and to sustain me in this new circumstance.

Therein is the conclusion of faithfulness. It is not that *we* are faithful; it is that *God* is faithful! It's not about our success; it's about his glory! So, as you head to your place of service may you cling to the promise of 1 Thessalonians 5:23–24: "Now may the God of peace himself sanctify you completely. And may your whole spirit, soul, and body be kept sound and blameless at the coming of our Lord Jesus Christ. He who calls you is faithful; he will do it."

ABIDING WELL AS A FAMILY

You can only say, "Speak, LORD, for your servant is listening" (1 Sam. 3:9) if you are actually listening. Likewise, we can't be faithful to accomplish his will according to his grace if we are not first abiding in Christ. Jesus says:

> "I am the vine; you are the branches. The one who remains in me and I in him produces much fruit, because you can do nothing without me. . . .
> You did not choose me, but I chose you. I appointed you to go and produce fruit and that your fruit should remain, so that whatever you ask the Father in my name, he will give you."
> (John 15:5, 16)

Faithful living is the outflow of an abiding life. We must guard the abiding life intentionally. Our family has worked hard to safeguard time together in family devotions. We first began with simple stories that our kids acted out and discussed. Later we worked through books of the Bible together. There came a time when I realized that my children were being fed too much through me and my wife and had not sufficiently developed the ability to feed themselves. So, we switched things up and let different children lead our family time. Now we settle on a book, do individual study, and then discuss what God has taught each of us after dinner. It's about more than devotions. These are the ongoing conversations that Moses encouraged in Deuteronomy 6:6–9. Abiding is not a time in the day but a lifestyle commitment.

What are the rhythms that you have already established in your life? When you arrive on the field, there are going to be a lot of things that will need to change to fit your context. Guard the abiding rhythms that you have established. As children of God, we have been gifted eternal life through Christ. Let us be diligent to walk in it. When we walk apart from Christ, there is no productivity, eternal fruit, lasting joy, or peace that surpasses understanding. Without Christ, our works are merely vain striving. Therefore, be sure to abide well.

Be faithful to give your spouse the time she needs to abide. Life on the field requires a lot of adaptation for wives and mothers. Cooking takes more time. Getting the language is particularly challenging for women who cannot get out in public as much due to the cultural context or family responsibilities. Her network of friends, confidants, and accountability partners is a world away. Help your wife protect the abiding rhythms that she needs. Carve out time for your spouse to enjoy regular times in the Word.

LEADING YOUR WIFE TO BE ON MISSION

If you are married, God did not call you to the mission field alone. Husbands and wives are called to live the missionary life together. I have never seen it work well when a wife has felt that her job was merely to support her husband in his calling to be a missionary. God places the call to missions in the heart of both husband and wife as they surrender to his will. Like Priscilla and Aquila, we are sent out as coworkers in the kingdom.

My wife and I jumped into language learning when we arrived in our new country. We met a teacher who spoke no English, and our supervisors left for a city four days' drive away. With a local university behind our house, I quickly found some young men who agreed to help me learn the language in exchange for meals with our family. In the evenings, my friends would arrive for dinner. Due to this arrangement, I began to outpace my wife in language, which naturally discouraged her.

Our uneven pace of learning changed when I arranged for a female university student named Odet from our local church to help Becky. They quickly became good friends. I would stay home with our son occasionally in order to send them off on their language adventures. Odet had many friends, many who needed to hear the gospel. Soon our evenings also included Becky's friends coming over for dinner and her sharing the gospel for the first time in the local language.

After learning the language, we arrived in our new home city in Northern Mozambique. We worked with a struggling group of local believers to reach the surrounding Muslim community. Our family grew from having two kids to adding a third. There was so much to do in this new ministry location to reach the overwhelming lostness. My days were full of survey trips, discipleship with local leaders, and learning to share the gospel with our people group.

Becky's days were full of keeping up with our growing family and doing everything it meant to live in Africa. She faithfully shared her faith with our houseworker and women who would come to the gate, but much of her energy during this season was focused on internal matters. Once again, my language grew by leaps and bounds, and I enjoyed that formative time in ministry by establishing key relationships and learning by experience.

Discouragement began to set in again with Becky. It was hard for her to see purpose amidst the frustrations of life and to keep focused without meaningful ministry opportunities outside the home. So we decided that I would take care of the kids on Fridays, and Becky would take the day to go out and engage in a ministry opportunity of her choosing. God moved so powerfully in that time. Becky saw the first person––a lady named Fatima––from our people group come to faith. Fatima formed her own group, which Becky helped to teach. The ladies loved her, and the time out in ministry renewed Becky's calling. Many gave their hearts to Christ.

Honestly, missionary life is full of joy and sorrow. It includes seasons of fruitful harvest and seasons of thankless sowing. As a husband, you will need to be intentional to help navigate the seasons of life for your family. You will need to affirm your wife in the seasons of hands-on motherhood, and you will have to provide calendar margin in the seasons where there is more opportunity for outward-facing ministry. It requires everything from your heart, your attention, and your energy, yet God provides beyond human limitation. Like my wife, Becky, your wife needs to experience all of missionary life. It will often be your job to look for ways to free her to participate in meaningful ministry outside the home. The effort is worth it, though, because together, God will set your hearts on fire and galvanize your calling.

LEADING YOUR KIDS TO BE ON MISSION

Your family is a blessing from God and your second greatest priority. God's first calling on your life is, of course, the calling to himself. However, if God has given you a wife and children, you have a great responsibility to steward these great blessings. As you do, they will be God-given instruments in your pursuit of Christlikeness. Loving them well, however, does not have to be separate from involving them in your calling to missionary life.

A common pitfall that can lead to missionary failure is accepting the "foray life." In foray life, some missionaries make forays into ministry work from within more comfortable social communities composed of other foreigners. After all, these people and places often provide the opportunities we want to give our children. To integrate into these ex-pat communities, though, housing is usually separate from the people you minister to, and local visitors are rare. Maintaining a comfortable homelife takes time, and children's schedules begin to fill with activities that take them further into the ex-pat community and further away from the target people. Visits into the local community are made to "do ministry," but language learning and the development of cultural savvy are stunted due to the majority of time being spent in the curated culture of the ex-pat community.

Foray life is what it looks like when being a missionary becomes a job. The foray life approach may appear reasonable because you are trying to provide the best life for your family, according to a Westerner's view of the "best life." But remember God's calling on your family's life. If you, as parents, trust God to be faithful to you through his calling to missions, you can also trust him to be faithful to the kids he has entrusted to your care. He will be faithful even if they do not have the same opportunities as their peers back home.

We have four kids—third culture kids (TCKs), as the experts call them. This means they are a unique blend of their parents' home culture and the culture where they grow up overseas. At the age of twelve, our eldest son decided he wanted to play soccer—football, as most of the world calls it. He joined the local team of older and more experienced players. At his first practice, he was so pitiful that his own team would take the ball away from him so he didn't lose possession to the opposing team. Undeterred, he continued to practice at 5:30 every morning in the village. Soon, his teammates walked him home, wanting to ensure the only foreigner in the league made it home safely. Friendships began to form, and his skills began to improve.

One day the dad of one of his friends died. My son and I went to the family house and attended the funeral. Years later, my son is in the United States and is an excellent soccer player. Two weeks ago, his local friend approached me and said, "I'll never forget the time you and Andrew came to my father's funeral. How is Andrew doing?" He started as a foreigner to be endured and became a friend through whom they heard about Christ.

My middle two kids, Dylan and Kate, are more introspective and can be more attuned to having insecurities about making mistakes. Still, when they were just eleven and nine, the Lord grew their courage as they decided to help a short-term missionary teach English in the local village. They worked in the local language as they taught. Of course, they made mistakes, but that was okay. The point wasn't to work perfectly, but to help others learn English. In each lesson, they faithfully presented the gospel and gave personal attention to their students. At the end of term, our house was full of students for an "English-only dinner" and games. To this day, people in the local village stop us and ask how teacher Dylan and teacher Kate are doing.

Each person in your family is different. Look for an avenue of ministry that fits how God has made them. As you look at those that God has given you to love and lead, be aware of how God has personally shaped them, and put them in positions where they can be successful. As a couple, we have enjoyed discussing how God has uniquely shaped our kids for this life. I would recommend having the same discussion with your wife.

MAKING TIME FOR WHAT MATTERS

Perhaps by now, you are getting excited about heading to the field as a couple and family. But, there is one more thing I want to mention before we conclude, and it's instrumental to everything else. If you do not intentionally make time for what matters, you will live a hectic life but fail to see the progress and fruit you long for.

Build your schedule around healthy rhythms. It is vital to have rhythms that help you and your family abide well. For example, you should prioritize a good rest rhythm. We have battled to protect a good rest pattern as a family because the Sabbath rhythm is biblical. You must be disciplined to have a Sabbath and learn the skill of scheduling in enough margin in your schedule. We have always struggled with being overly optimistic in our planning and not giving enough margin for the inefficiencies of living on the field.

Walking in a manner worthy of your calling also means being faithful in your ministry rhythms. Being a missionary is hard work. Biblical transformation takes time. You have been called to "make disciples of all nations" (Matt. 28:19) and to pour yourself out in worship as God pours into you. Guard your time in making disciples zealously. The mission God is sending you on will probably take years. Don't be lulled into a sense of complacency.

Our mission is also urgent. We don't have time to waste on what is merely good. We have to discern and be committed to what is best. There will be many demands on our time, such as meetings, trainings, cohorts, logistical needs, and requests of your time from your organization and community. Ensure you are faithful to protect your time for your personal walk, marriage, family life, and the ministry God has given you to the people he has sent you. Remember to begin with the end in mind. Are you being faithful?

Sure, they are going to pick up some parasites along the way. It's worth it. Our kids knew and felt proud that they were part of the team, serving the Lord together as a family. They will view the world in ways that are different from their peers back home. They will understand the global family of God in ways that will expand their vision of God's kingdom. For instance, our kids were baptized alongside their African brothers and sisters. They have seen God do miraculous things. They have seen the kingdom of Satan defeated before their very eyes by the power of the gospel and the name of Jesus. Rather than seeing what your kids are missing out on from life back home, joyfully and gratefully consider and recount the myriad blessings that they are exposed to as they are integrated into your life of ministry.

DISCUSS AND REFLECT

1. What is your current rhythm for abiding personally, in your marriage, and in your family? How can you protect that rhythm on the field?

2. How will you negotiate the rigors of missionary life to make time for both of you to be faithful in your calling as disciples, spouses, parents, and missionaries?

3. As you look at your children, what might be some opportunities that you foresee for them to be on mission and in the community with mom and dad?

4. What has work life/homelife looked like for you and your wife in the States? How do you typically divide up the various family responsibilities between the two of you? What do you anticipate

changing to accommodate both of your ministries when you live overseas?

5. What are some of the expectations you have on "family time" going into overseas ministry? What will work look like for you? How will you make time for and include your family in ministry?

CHAPTER 9

Suffering and the Missionary Life

Brooks Buser

From the General Editor

BEFORE YOU GO, you need to consider the cost. You need to consider the fact that suffering and gospel advance are tightly interwoven in the history of the church. Like others working out their missionary calling, you have probably heard the stories of suffering, and thought, *I could never do that*. If your eyes are on yourself, you will naturally feel weak and inadequate in the face of physical trials and spiritually hard hearts.

I (Josh) invite you to sit with our friend Brooks Buser as he shares his story of leaving a successful business career to take the gospel to the Yembiyembi people. Brooks had to ask some of the hardest questions when confronted with the sickness of his own children—times when he didn't know if they would survive.

In this chapter, Brooks carefully points us to a sufficient Savior who is worth sacrificial living. Brooks lived for years among an unreached people group in a primitive setting. His family learned the language and worked to translate the Bible into the local language. He was also blessed to see a church formed and leaders prepared among the Yembiyembi. Brooks is now president of Radius International, which trains men and women to go to unreached language groups to plant healthy local churches.

I invite you to be amazed at God's faithfulness to Brooks's family as they endured many hardships. More than that, I ask you to remember the simple disciplines that send down deep roots of trust in our sovereign Lord. I invite you to remember that suffering in this life is expected, as we often read in the New Testament. It is probably better that you don't know all you will face as you walk this road of obedience. Brooks and I would encourage you to lean on the One who is faithful and remember that he is all you need.

WHAT IF . . . ?

As we rounded the second to last bend in the river before reaching the village, the distinct sound of the mission airplane suddenly flashed overhead. Our hunting party had a great day (three wild boars and one cassowary), and we were all in high spirits. But that all changed suddenly with the sound of the Cessna 206 coming in at such a low altitude—indicating they were landing at our small airfield because something had turned in my son's health. For weeks my six-year-old son, Beau, had been fighting a fever, and no matter what medication we gave him, he was unable to shake his sickness. So, the mission doctors recommended we give it one more week before traveling to see them in person, unless his fever spiked above 103. Then we would need to medevac immediately.

SUFFERING AND THE MISSIONARY LIFE

The motor canoe driver, Taliogol ("Skip," as the kids called him), saw my look and twisted the handle on the outboard 40 hp motor to the fastest notch of speed, and we flew up the final bend of the Salumei River. The motor canoe emerged into the open section of the river, just below the village to our right and the airfield to our left, as the plane lumbered into the parking area. Skip skillfully aimed the nose of the long motor canoe toward the bank, and we began jumping out of our canoe as soon as it had wedged itself to a stop in the thick mud at the riverbank.

My wife, Nina, was holding Beau, and we quickly hugged as she brought me up to speed. His fever had spiked to 105 in the last four hours, and by God's grace, the mission plane was flying in the area and had space for two. I quickly did the math and realized they would be going, and I would be staying behind. The Yembiyembi believers (having heard the gospel just a few months earlier) and I prayed a quick prayer as we loaded Nina and Beau on the plane—and just like that, the prop was spinning and the aircraft was moving. I watched as the red and white plane went to the end of the grass runway, revved up, and lifted off into the late afternoon sun of Papua New Guinea.

Two days later, the plane would make it back into our area, and I would fly out to our mission base to see Beau begin the recovery process. Unfortunately, he had contracted a rare form of malaria. After two weeks at our mission base, he fully recovered, and we began planning to fly back into Yembiyembi. That's when the second-guessing started. We had made it out this time, but what if he got the same sickness again, and it was worse? What if the plane wasn't in the area next time? *What if . . . ?*

THE GOSPEL'S ADVANCE AND SUFFERING

Before Nina and I went into missions, I worked as a chief financial officer (CFO) for a Dutch manufacturing company. We enjoyed many of the perks of life in San Diego, California, and were on our way to an early retirement. But, in the grace of God, we saw clearly in Scripture something better to give our lives to, and our plans were rerouted to Papua New Guinea, and eventually, the Yembiyembi people. Every step of that departure process was a painful loss. We grieved leaving our home church, my job, our family, and San Diego. This pain was like a slow "dying" we went through. Each time the pain of losing the familiar or the safety net was a jarring removal of a comfort we had so cherished.

Paul observes something similar in his words to the Corinthian church in 2 Corinthians 4:7–12:

> Now we have this treasure in clay jars, so that this extraordinary power may be from God and not from us. We are afflicted in every way but not crushed; we are perplexed but not in despair; we are persecuted but not abandoned; we are struck down but not destroyed. We always carry the death of Jesus in our body, so that the life of Jesus may also be displayed in our body. For we who live are always being given over to death for Jesus's sake, so that Jesus's life may also be displayed in our mortal flesh. So then, death is at work in us, but life in you.

SUFFERING AND THE MISSIONARY LIFE

This "dying" was necessary so we could fully give ourselves to gospel ministry among our people/language group. And this dying was something we would start to observe throughout our ministry overseas. We were dying to our rights, comfort, safety, and sounding smart and educated. This went on for years, especially during our language-learning period! We quickly realized these challenges were not one-time events to hurdle so we could get back to normal. No. This was a lifestyle that we would be getting used to, a new normal.

By our fifth year in Papua New Guinea, I had contracted malaria seven times, and Nina had a running battle with tropical boils that would last for years. We had lost our dear co-workers in the ministry early on in those years as they returned home, and the weight of the task was heavy on us. God had sustained us through all these things, but the price tag was increasingly costly. I remember reading John Piper's introduction to *Filling Up the Afflictions* (now part of the book *27 Servants of Sovereign Joy*), where he says, "More and more I am persuaded from Scripture and from the history of missions that God's design for the evangelization of the world and the consummation of his purposes includes the suffering of his ministers and missionaries."[22] I think he's right.

Our own experience and countless missionary biographies testify that there is a direct relationship between the gospel's advance and the suffering of those who carry that gospel message. For example, many people know Amy Carmichael's writing but are unaware her influential books were written while she was bedridden for the final twenty years of her life. Many know of John Paton's ministry among the previously cannibalistic people of the New Hebrides (now called Vanuatu) without remembering how he lost his wife and child during their first year. Adoniram Judson produced an incredible Bible translation in Burma, but was subjected to brutal imprisonment, lost two wives, endured the death of seven children, and fought severe bouts of depression.

Suffering and the advance of the gospel walk hand in hand. I am regularly encouraged by the words the apostle Paul penned in 2 Corinthians 4:16–18 that show how missionaries have coped with such suffering and pressed on. Paul opens with all the people that are getting saved and how the gospel is resulting in praise to God. Then he says this:

> Therefore we do not give up. Even though our outer person is being destroyed, our inner person is being renewed day by day. For our momentary light affliction is producing for us an absolutely incomparable eternal weight of glory. So we do not focus on what is seen, but on what is unseen. For what is seen is temporary, but what is unseen is eternal.

Yes, suffering is real, and it's painful. Anyone who tries to downplay the goodbyes, the sickness, the drudgery of language-learning, and all the other challenging aspects of missionary life is not living in reality. The apostle Paul doesn't try to minimize these things. He fully acknowledges them, but he also acknowledges the greater reality: the Christ follower is a stranger in this world, belonging to a different country (Heb. 11:13–16).

Paul is saying something quite powerful in labeling his sufferings "momentary" and "light" (2 Cor. 4:17). Remember that *five times* Paul endured the forty lashes minus one, was beaten by rods three times, stoned once, and shipwrecked three times (11:24–25). And he says these are merely *momentary* and *light*! How does he assign such pain and suffering this weightless label? The only way he can assign suffering this label is because he saw past this world. He saw past the whips, shipwrecks, and physical pain. He recognized there was a greater reality that his physical eyes could not see that was just as real.

Look at how Paul contrasts these realities. One is destroying our outward person, and one is renewing our inner person each day. One is "light," and the other has "weight." One is "momentary," and the other is "eternal." One is easily seen, and the other is unseen (4:16–18). The suffering that goes hand in hand with missionary work is not only bearable but also brings joy! Not because missionaries live in some Pollyanna, glib, twisted reality, but because they recognize the reality that supersedes all realities; namely, these four things: (1) I am a temporary resident on this earth; (2) what I do with my short life here carries significant weight in the life to come; (3) my King will never abandon me; and (4) I am nearly home.

So how does someone latch on to those eternal realities as they prepare to walk the path of the missionary? Let me offer four bits of practical advice.

KNOW YOUR BIBLE WELL

It is no overstatement to say that this is the most vital relationship someone should have in place before heading to the field. I say "relationship" because someone who persistently reads, studies, and memorizes the Scriptures is almost invariably in close communion with the Author of Scripture—the God of heaven and earth. New believers tend to devour their Bible and get excited at each new truth they see. By God's grace, those who have walked the path of the Christian life longer can still be excited by the truths in Scripture, but they also have a track record of seeing how their God has used those truths to steer their path in life.

Healthy churches are the best environment to get to know the Bible. Missionaries who know their Bible well will be better translators, teachers of the Word, and better coworkers. A relationship with God, built through a knowledge of his Word, will not let them down when suffering comes. Through hard goodbyes, sicknesses, culture shock/stress, loneliness, and all types of suffering, the Lord will be with them "to the very end of the age" (Matt. 28:20 NIV).

The older I have gotten, the more I realize that the "sword" (Heb. 4:12) is not the paper-and-print Bible—it is memorized Scripture. The Scripture you have treasured, stored up, and studied is the surest bulwark against the testing the Enemy will surely put you through. Jesus in his wilderness temptation, Paul when he gave his impromptu teaching on Mars Hill, Stephen as he was about to be stoned, and so many others had the word buried in their hearts and minds. Aspiring missionaries will do well to treasure the Word in their hearts (Ps. 119:11) for the wind and waves that are surely coming. Missionary life is one of incredible triumph and crushing hardship—equally allowed by the hand of Christ. There is no substitute in those hard times for the Word of God etched in the mind and ready on the lips.

READ GOOD BOOKS

When I step into the first day of teaching classes at Radius,[23] a nine-month missionary training school, I try to ascertain who my "readers" are and who my "aspiring readers" are. There is no third category of "nonreaders." Yes, some people have a harder time reading. Still, all of us have the capacity to get written material into our heads through structure (five minutes a day for some), creativity (audiobooks), and dogged determination. What awaits those who crack good books are incredible treasures that will sustain them on their earthly pilgrimage.

I wish so badly I had read more missionary biographies before I went to the field. *Amy Carmichael: Beauty for Ashes* by Iain H. Murray, *To the Golden Shore: The Life of Adoniram Judson* by Courtney Anderson, *Five Pioneer Missionaries* edited by S. M. Houghton (an excellent book for single guys), *The Autobiography of John Paton*, *The St. Andrews Seven* by Stuart Piggin and John Roxborogh (how a good teacher affects missionaries), *The Autobiography of Hudson Taylor*, *27 Servants of Sovereign Joy: Faithful, Flawed, and Fruitful* by John Piper (short biographies), and *A Chance to Die: The Life and Legacy of Amy Carmichael* by Elisabeth Elliot (great for ladies) are great starting points. Missionary biographies have this potent effect in strengthening Christians for suffering. We are able to zoom out and see the totality of the person's life and how they trusted God in their darkest hours. Every missionary will go through seasons of suffering. The great benefit of reading good biographies is that they allow us to see things with a better perspective and give us solid hope that we will see the other side.

The other significant aspect of missionary biographies is that they give tangible examples. One of Satan's most potent lies is that we are alone, and no one else has suffered the way we are. Stories of saints from previous generations shatter that lie. They point to frail, weak, often wounded people that trust in their God to the very end. They teach us that we are *not* alone; others have endured the same types of suffering—and many to a greater extent—which gives us the courage to press on. Missionary biographies are an excellent source of strength in preparation for and during times of suffering.

Other books that I would highly recommend for aspiring missionaries would be:

- *Let the Nations Be Glad!: The Supremacy of God in Missions*—John Piper (the gold standard for understanding the "why" of missions)
- *What Is the Mission of the Church?: Making Sense of Social Justice, Shalom, and the Great Commission*—Kevin DeYoung and Greg Gilbert (What *is* and *isn't* missions . . . so good!)
- *Precious Remedies Against Satan's Devices*—Thomas Brooks (how to stand strong in hard times)
- *Strength for the Weary*—Derek W. H. Thomas (the comfort of God to the weak and weary)

SUFFERING AND THE MISSIONARY LIFE

- *These Strange Ashes*—Elisabeth Elliot (God is good through suffering)
- *Holiness*—J. C. Ryle—(how to live as a Christian . . . so good!)
- *If God is Good: Faith in the Midst of Suffering and Evil*—Randy Alcorn (If God is good, why do we suffer so much?)
- *Evangelism and the Sovereignty of God*—J. I. Packer (God saves sinners; what a relief!)
- *The Bruised Reed*—Richard Sibbes (Christ is gentle and kind with hurting people.)
- *No Shortcut to Success: A Manifesto for Modern Missions*—Matt Rhodes (why missionaries should be qualified and proficient, for the sake of the gospel and the church)
- *Don't Waste Your Life*—John Piper (maybe the best book to give to a Christian in high school/college)
- *Twelve Ordinary Men: How the Master Shaped His Disciples for Greatness, and What He Wants to Do with You*—John MacArthur (the apostles after Christ returned to heaven and the price they paid)
- *Suffering and the Sovereignty of God*—John Piper and Justin Taylor (God is all-powerful and still allows suffering)

Aspiring missionaries, cultivate the habit of reading good books. They will help you the most when the storm of life is the fiercest.

KEEP A JOURNAL

While I'm sure this may be tough for some to swallow, this discipline has proven encouraging in hard times. Journaling is not a female-only endeavor; it's a helpful tool for anyone who wants to have a record of how God has dealt with them. I was skeptical of this discipline until I started, then after a few months, I reread some of my original entries.

I learned how I thought, understood God, and handled pressure over time. Looking at what I put to paper (mine are actually on the computer) a year ago, or even ten years ago, is a great encouragement. We can see God's good hand in sanctifying us. The greatest value in journaling, though, comes not in seeing your growth but in seeing the faithful kindness of your God. Human beings are prone to forget. We remember pain quite well, but we tend to forget when the answers to hard questions, relief from pain, and kindness in unexpected ways come to us.

A few years after the medevac incident with Beau, I was reading through my journal again and remembered the feelings of helplessness, fear, and eventual relief. Those moments strengthened my faith. But that written record—the details that are so easily lost to time—is there and still teaching me lessons today. A record of God's goodness to us can hearten us and shape us in ways few other things can.

BE A FAITHFUL CHURCH MEMBER

God made Christians to live in community. We are saved individually from our sins but into a community, tribe, body, and group that shares our same eternal hope. That group is called the church. Missionaries tend to be hard chargers, especially missionaries to unreached language groups. This is a good thing. You need to have a certain level of grit, toughness, or drive to get to some challenging places and live there for long periods. But the downside is that this kind of individual or couple can fall into the thinking that they don't need the church. But the Bible and church history knows nothing of missionaries who were not first faithful church members.

The Scriptures teach us that it is normally the church that baptizes new believers (Matt. 28:19), it is the church that practices the Lord's Supper (1 Cor. 10:16–17; 11:23–28), it is through the church that the wisdom of God is made known to the world (Eph. 3:10), and it is the church that Christ will return for someday (Titus 2:13). The church is the epicenter of all that God is doing on the earth. To be lukewarm to the church, to think church attendance is optional, weakens a person more than they know. A church may not be available in frontier missionary settings, thus the reason that someone is going there. But, the people of God will always carry with them the natural and good inclination to gather with other people who love the Lord Jesus.

Listen to Peter's advice to the Christians of his time who were facing fierce persecution:

> Be sober-minded; be watchful. Your adversary the devil prowls around like a roaring lion,

seeking someone to devour. Resist him, firm in your faith, knowing that the same kinds of suffering are being experienced by your brotherhood throughout the world. (1 Pet. 5:8–9 ESV)

Peter says that we draw strength to fight through trials not from ourselves, but from the knowledge of our brothers who are going through the same things, from our fellow church members all around the world. When a person is part of a regular gathering of believers, they find community, strength, and the environment they were created for as a Christian.

The persecution was quite intense in the early days of the Yembiyembi church. The first baptism of seven people was attended by the entire village of nearly a thousand people. Most adamantly opposed the baptisms; some even came with spears against those baptized. The early believers had gardens destroyed and houses cut down, and some were physically beaten. Several times I was warned of an ambush waiting for me on the trail home. Finally, when the tension was at its worst, Nina and Beau had to be flown out.

But oh, the sweetness of those early days when we would gather as a church! It's hard to find words to express what a tangible outpost of heaven those gatherings were. We sang, prayed, heard the Word taught, gathered in the name of our triune God, and rejoiced that our Savior had counted us worthy of his glory. And slowly, the church began to grow. Unbelievers wanted to see what was so special that we would return Sunday after Sunday. That testimony, the testimony of the church, has continued to this day to win many to Christ. The power of the regular Sunday gathering of Christians is matchless in its testimony to the world and encouragement to Christians going through suffering.

FOLLOWING IN FAITH

After Beau came back to full health, we boarded that same small Cessna and made our way back into Yembiyembi. We would live and work there for seven more years to see the church brought to full maturity. Beau would contract malaria three more times during those seven years and go through other health issues that kept Nina and me on our knees through long, dark nights. But we never doubted the goodness of our God. The verses we had stashed away in our minds came like bursts of cold water when we needed them most. We never regretted attending a Christian college and the additional Bible and practical training that was poured into us through our two years of training before leaving for Papua New Guinea. We thanked the Lord regularly for a home church that kept up with us and prayed with us through many dark and lonely nights, and then eventually, to see the Yembiyembi church planted and come to maturity. It is one of my life's sweetest blessings. I have occasionally gone back and reread what I had put down to paper about that period and been reminded afresh how kind God was—and is—to us.

It's never easy to walk away from home, family, job, and the safety of a known environment. But the God of the ages has promised that what is unseen and eternal far outweighs all we may go through in this momentary world. And someday our faith will be made sight, and all things will be made new. We live for that day.

DISCUSS AND REFLECT

1. Have you thought through what the cost of going into missions may be for you?

2. Are there "untouchable" areas in your life that, if the Lord pressed, would cause you to turn back?

3. Have you talked through those areas with your spouse and church leaders?

4. Do you have the rock-solid conviction that your God is always good?

5. Do you know where you will turn when the storms of life come?

CHAPTER 10

The Spiritual Life of a Missionary

Zane Pratt

From the General Editor

AS A FORMER International Mission Board missionary, I (Josh) grew to respect the theological conviction and missiological clarity of our vice president for global training, Zane Pratt. He was instrumental in writing the *Foundations* resource book that carefully defines key terms and the core missionary tasks. I believe his careful stewardship of his role has been an asset to this influential missions organization.

Zane served as a missionary in Central Asia before eventually serving in various leadership roles. Based on his leadership, experience, and faithfulness over several decades, I believe he can speak well to the issue of success and longevity as a missionary. Zane has interviewed hundreds of new missionary candidates and visited just as many in their place of service. He is also aware of the many reasons that missionaries fail, come home early, or are disqualified.

In this chapter, Zane returns to the themes of abiding and the local church that have been prevalent throughout this book.

Before you go, don't overlook the critical nature of your own spiritual life because it appears simple or obvious. Don't allow the urgency of others' spiritual needs to cause you to neglect your own need for continual connection to Christ. I am grateful for Zane's wisdom, clarity, and straightforward words, and I trust they lead you to rest and abide in the Vine.

DISCONNECTED AND BURNED OUT

Richard was going back to the United States. After four years on the field, he was exhausted and burned out. He had entered his country with high expectations of people saved, believers discipled, churches planted, and leaders trained. He had applied himself diligently to language learning and to understanding the culture of his people group. He had shared the gospel faithfully. His days, evenings, and weekends were filled with activity as he led Bible studies, organized new churches, and trained leaders. He had even seen some measure of fruit. However, at the end of his first term, he was done. He had nothing left to give.

What had led to this disappointing conclusion to his short missionary career? Very simply, he had substituted activity for Christ in the place of abiding in Christ. He had worked for God but not walked with God. His calendar had been full, but his soul was empty. He had somehow believed the hype that missionaries are super-saints who don't need the same routine disciplines as ordinary believers. He had pursued God's work on his own strength, leaving him powerless and ready to quit.

Churches in North America put missionaries on a pedestal. They are regarded as the Special Forces of the body of Christ.

THE SPIRITUAL LIFE OF A MISSIONARY

Time and again, missionary candidates and missionaries on furlough are told by their fellow church members how brave and committed they are. This is often accompanied by the solemn statement: "I could never do that!" Ordinary Christians assume that it takes an extraordinary spiritual life to serve in missions, so anyone who is a missionary must have such an extraordinary spiritual life. This assumption can rub off on the missionaries themselves. The experience of being sent to the field (or sent back to the field after furlough) can be heady, as you bask in the glow of commissioning services and sending celebrations. It is easy to start to believe the hype. Everyone around you thinks you are a super-saint, so it must be true, right?

THE VINE AND THE BRANCHES

Jesus thought otherwise. Speaking to the apostles whom he had trained, and on whose testimony and labors he would build his church, Jesus said:

> "I am the true vine, and my Father is the gardener. Every branch in me that does not produce fruit he removes, and he prunes every branch that produces fruit so that it will produce more fruit. You are already clean because of the word I have spoken to you. Remain in me, and I in you. Just as a branch is unable to produce fruit by itself unless it remains on the vine, neither can you unless you remain in me. I am the vine; you are the branches. The one who remains in me

and I in him produces much fruit, because you can do nothing without me." (John 15:1–5)

The setting for this passage is the conversation Jesus had with his disciples the night before he was crucified. His message was laced with some of the most important themes of his ministry. He spoke of faith, love, and obedience. In addition, he gave some of the clearest teaching in the New Testament on the person and work of the Holy Spirit, whom he would send to them after he had gone. John 15 is a rich passage that rewards careful and repeated study. In the middle of this charge, Jesus introduced the image of vines and branches and the subject of abiding in him. It is worth a closer look, because it speaks perfectly to the necessity of the spiritual life of a missionary.

The image of vines and branches is easy to picture. In Jesus's day, everyone lived near or participated in agriculture. Anyone understands that if you cut a branch from its vine, it dies. The vine can exist without the branch, but the branch cannot survive without the vine. The vine provides sustenance for the branch, which the branch must have to live. So it is with us as disciples of Jesus. As Jesus said succinctly, apart from him, we can do nothing (v. 5). We are as dependent on Jesus as a branch is on its vine. If we are cut off from him, we wither and die.

In many ways, of course, we can do a great deal apart from Jesus. We can generate a lot of activity and produce impressive-looking "results" relying on our own resources. However, none of it will have eternal significance. It is highly unlikely to last. And we ourselves, dependent on our own strength, will wither just like a cut-off branch.

BEARING FRUIT

In this passage, Jesus links abiding in him to bearing fruit. What kind of fruit does he have in mind? In the New Testament, the word *fruit* is used several ways. One, obviously, is the fruit of a literal plant, but this passage clearly uses the term metaphorically. One metaphorical use of fruit simply refers to the consequences of someone's life, whether good or bad. "You'll recognize them by their fruit," said Jesus in the Sermon on the Mount (Matt. 7:16), referring to the difference between true and false prophets. In Galatians, Paul utilizes this positively to refer to the fruit of the Spirit. When the Holy Spirit is active in the life of Christian disciples, their character and behavior are changed as he makes them more and more like Christ, and these transformations are enumerated in Galatians 5:22–23. This list describes who Jesus is and who Jesus's disciples are becoming as the Spirit conforms them to the image of God, displayed perfectly for us in God the Son Incarnate.

The fruit of the Spirit is the key to any other kind of fruit-bearing. The goal of discipleship is to be conformed to Christ's image and equipped for Christ's work, and without the first, the second will be meaningless. You must be a disciple to make disciples, and disciples demonstrate the fruit of the Spirit in growing measure in their lives. The fruit of the Spirit produces in the context of abiding in Christ. For disciples of Jesus to bear the fruit of a transformed life that honors and reflects God, they must remain intimate with Christ.

Another meaning of fruit in the New Testament is the results of your ministry. Every missionary goes to the field yearning to see things happen. They long to see lost people pass from death to life by believing the Good News of the gospel. They yearn to see believers grow into mature disciples. They desire to see healthy churches planted and grown to maturity. They yearn to see well-trained, godly leaders raised up for these churches. This kind of fruit is the desire of every missionary. But, in this passage, Jesus tells us that we will not bear this kind of fruit apart from abiding in him.

SUCCESS, FAITHFULNESS, AND PRUNING

You do not know what kind of ministry fruit you will bear. Success in missions is faithfulness to Christ and faithfulness in the task, not numerical results. God is sovereign; we are not, and our ministry results are in his hands. However, we should all expect the fruit of growing Christlikeness, and in God's good timing, we can also expect the gospel to bear its fruit among the lost.

Here is the rub. As Jesus said clearly in this passage from John's Gospel, God may need to prune you for you to bear fruit (John 15:2). Pruning can be profoundly uncomfortable, and our flesh craves comfort. However, as all of us who have engaged in this work for any length of time can testify, we have been pruned, we are still being pruned, and pruning is usually painful.

Pruning for a missionary can take several forms. It involves being reduced to a position of less communication competence than the average three-year-old as you embark on language-learning. It involves removing your cultural and social props as you plunge into cross-cultural adjustment and experience culture shock. It involves confronting your sin like never before—especially sins like selfishness, entitlement, and irritability. In some settings, it may involve physical discomfort and lingering sickness. It often includes complicated team relationships as you find yourself bound to others like never before. At all times, the pruning involves outright spiritual warfare, as the Enemy of our souls vents his hatred toward our God on us.

You are in for a season of pruning as you engage in this work. It is crucially important that you keep two things in mind. First, whether the pruning comes via language-learning, the local culture, sickness, or even the Enemy himself, it comes from the hand of God. He intends it for our good and his glory. Whatever our God sends our way is good and right, and he is using these afflictions as a surgeon's scalpel or a gardener's shears, pruning away what is unlike him in our lives. Second, it is worth it. It is not easy, but the fruit will be sweet. Be prepared for the best, most challenging season of your life.

ABIDING IN THE WORD AND PRAYER

So what does it mean to abide in Christ? Jesus tells us that it includes his Word abiding in us (v. 7). Scripture is one of the most important of the gracious tools God has given us to pursue intimacy with him and grow in his likeness. If you are going to abide in him and bear fruit, you must hear, read, study, memorize, and meditate on Scripture as a nonnegotiable component of your life. You need daily time in the Word like you need your daily bread. The goal is more than acquiring a store of Bible trivia. Reading or hearing the Bible does not give you automatic merit as in some religious systems. Rather, the goal is a transformed mind. The word of God needs to reshape our worldview such that we look at everything through the lens of God's truth. Our conception of reality, our values, our affections, and our behaviors all need to be remade by Scripture. This will not happen through occasional or casual time in the Word. The world is constantly propagandizing us, trying to reshape our worldview in its likeness. We need Bible input daily to clean our minds and restore our sanity.

In addition to the Word, abiding in Christ requires all the traditional spiritual disciplines of the Christian life. It includes a deep commitment to prayer. This does not simply mean praying before meals or before going to bed. It is more than even extended prayer times every day, although that is essential. Scripture commands us to "pray without ceasing" (1 Thess. 5:17 ESV). This does not mean having a quiet time that lasts twenty-four hours a day. Instead, it means going through the day in constant conversation with God, thanking him for every blessing, and turning to him in every situation. Prayer is the life-giving breath of the Christian life. It is how we walk in fellowship with God, demonstrating our dependence on God. Prayerlessness may be the most common mistake missionaries make, but it is fatal. Prayer is not a distraction from our work. On the contrary, it is the lifeblood of the missionary task and deserves top priority on our schedules.

THANKSGIVING

One type of prayer deserves separate mention, and that is thanksgiving. An older missionary colleague observed that there are two types of missionaries (and really, two types of Christians): those who are thankful, and those who are entitled. Entitlement comes easily to sinners like us. However, it is a deadly frame of mind. A spirit of entitlement leads missionaries to make their obedience conditional on having a certain level of housing, transportation, budget, or some other tangible benefit. Entitled people are seldom content and frequently complain. The best antidote for entitlement is gratitude.

The missionary (or any Christian, actually) who is full of gratitude realizes that neither God nor the universe owes us anything. Such missionaries grasp that every good thing we enjoy comes from God, as a gift of his grace, and they are grateful for what they have rather than resentful for what they don't have. The best way to cultivate gratitude is to get in the habit of thanking God for everything. A grateful missionary goes through the day thanking God for necessities such as food, shelter, clothing, and extraordinary blessings such as gospel opportunities and spiritual fruit. Thanksgiving is one of the healthiest disciplines a missionary can cultivate.

SELF-DENIAL

Abiding in Christ also entails times of self-denial and fasting. There are no set rules for how often or how long believers should fast, but both Jesus and the apostles assumed fasting and practiced it. Fasting is a lost art in the modern evangelical world, but it is a practice we must recover. When we fast, we remind ourselves that God is better than food or drink. He is better than life itself. Fasting humbles us before God, and humility is something every Christian needs to cultivate! Fasting also clears time for prayer and meditation on God's Word.

Jesus warns us of the danger of fasting to be seen by others, and we should beware of showing off our piety to impress others (Matt. 6:16–18). However, for most modern Christians, the temptation is not to seek the applause of people in our spiritual disciplines; the danger is to be so averse to discomfort that we simply never fast. For the sake of abiding in Christ, build fasting into your regular spiritual rhythms.

COMMITTED ENGAGEMENT IN A LOCAL CHURCH

Things like Bible study, prayer, thanksgiving, and fasting are individual spiritual disciplines, and many people only think of their spiritual lives in individualistic terms. These things should characterize the private life of missionaries, but they should also be practiced in the corporate life of the church. Every Christian needs the local church, and missionaries are no exception. God designed the church as the place where discipleship and maturity happen.

Some missionaries may think that they have an exalted calling that puts them above the need for the accountability, worship, or teaching of a church, but they are dangerously mistaken. The New Testament has no conception of a Christian who is not in a committed relationship with a particular body of believers, and that is just as true of missionaries as any other Christian.

Furthermore, membership in a sending church halfway around the world does not meet missionaries' need for church. Church happens where you are. Church is more than an event. It is a set of committed relationships, organized according to God's Word, in which God is worshiped, the Word is taught, the ordinances are observed, and the one-another commands of the

Bible are carried out. It should be a place where people know one another well enough to speak fruitfully into one another's lives.

For this reason, missionaries must engage in meaningful church membership on the field where they live. This is sometimes difficult due to the itinerant nature of some missionaries' jobs. In those situations, it is even more necessary, for the worker's health and well-being, that a local church takes responsibility for their soul. So, when you get to the field, either find or start a church and go deep in your involvement with it.

THE POINT OF SPIRITUAL DISCIPLINES

These are the essential elements of the spiritual life of a missionary: the Word of God, prayer, thanksgiving, fasting, and the life of a local church. One more observation is necessary, however. It is easy for us to turn our spiritual disciplines into a checklist of good works we do to stay on God's good side. They can become ends in themselves, or even worse, ways to earn God's favor. That is not the point of these disciplines at all. They are gifts of God; he gave them to us as ways to draw near to him. The point is intimacy with God, not check marks on a list of obligations. They are ways we can abide in Christ, and as we do so, they are also ways he reshapes us to be more like himself and equips us to carry out his mission in the world. So do not be content to do them as a religious obligation. Instead, use them to seek fellowship with God.

At the same time, it is better to exercise the spiritual disciplines with a dry spirit than not to do them at all. We all go through periods in our lives where it seems we are simply going through the motions. When that happens, do not succumb to the temptation to put off your devotional life or church involvement until you feel like it. Feelings can lie.

One bit of advice we gave our children over and over again was this: "You don't have to act the way you feel. Do what's right, whether you feel like it or not." This is true in every area of life, and it is crucially important in the area of spiritual disciplines. God often uses the dry seasons of our spiritual lives to grow our faith the most. So keep using the means of grace God has given you, whether you feel like it or not, and whether you feel like you are getting anything out of it or not. God is doing his gracious work in our lives through his gifts of the spiritual disciplines as much in the dry seasons as at any other time.

ORDINARY FAITHFULNESS

You are not a super-saint. Whatever others may say, the hype is not true. You are not above the need for Bible study, prayer, thanksgiving, fasting, or the local church. You desperately need intimacy with Christ. If you fill your calendar with ministry activity but do not stay close to him, you will end up like Richard, burned out and ready to quit.

For every negative example like Richard, many other field workers have made their time with God their highest priority. These are the people who have lasted in their service to Christ, and these are the ones who have borne fruit. These are also the ones who have counted their missionary service as a joy rather than an exhausting burden.

So abide in Christ. Don't let busyness pull you away from time with him, both alone and in the company of your church. Don't make the mistake of thinking that your work for God can ever replace your walk with God. Make it your priority. Put it in your schedule. Guard it jealously. When Jesus said that "apart from [him] you can do nothing" (John 15:5 ESV), he meant it. Don't be a casualty because you neglected intimacy with Christ. Instead, use the gracious means God has given you to cultivate your relationship with him. Make him your greatest treasure, and invest your time in all the ways he has given you to grow deep in faith, love, and obedience toward him.

DISCUSS AND REFLECT

1. Has there been a time in your life you have pursued ministry in your own strength? What happened?

2. What are you doing now to pursue intimacy with Christ? How faithful and consistent are you in these practices?

3. Are there things mentioned in this chapter you could either start doing or strengthen?

4. What is most likely to pull you away from your spiritual disciplines? How can you combat these temptations or distractions?

5. Do you think of spiritual disciplines as a checklist of things to please God rather than as gracious means God has given you to draw close to him? How can you recognize this tendency and work against it?

Conclusion

Josh Bowman

IF YOU HAVE reached this conclusion, you have likely worked your way through the various chapters preceding it. I think it is fair to say that, at this point, the authors of this book hope that you are feeling overwhelmed. Now, hang with us for a moment. We don't want you to be overwhelmed by the challenges, circumstances, or feelings of inadequacy that you are undoubtedly facing. Instead, we pray that you are absolutely overwhelmed by the power, provision, and grace of our faithful Savior. We pray you would be overwhelmed by the reality that he calls, equips, and sends us as ambassadors to partner in his mission. We all want you to remember that "He who calls you is faithful; he will do it" (1 Thess. 5:24). Awe and faith in God will enable us to view any future problems we face and people with whom we interact with a proper perspective.

Matt and I have commended each of these men to you as both examples and experts. At the same time, each contributor would admit to weaknesses, frailties, and frequent stumbles in our journeys. As you prepare to close this book and apply it to your ministry, I hope we have encouraged you to look to the Lord, who is our Helper (Ps. 121). Throughout Scripture, we find that God's presence with God's people comforts and empowers them to accomplish his purposes.

If you have feelings of inadequacy for the task God is calling you to, then you are in good company. Each contributor has, in his own way, faced circumstances that he feared were impossible or overwhelming. We have also been tempted to trust in ourselves, leading regularly to pride and, perhaps just as often, to feelings of inadequacy. Thankfully, God has a history of using what is broken and weak to ensure he gets the glory, not us.

As you continue your own walk of faith in obedience to God's call on your life, we trust these words have helped align your expectations with what you will experience shortly. We hope that the chapters stimulated many fruitful conversations with mentors and other Christians. We trust this resource has complemented your theological education and local church training.

We wish that, as you close this book, we could literally be getting up from your dining room table after the second cup of coffee to shake your hand as we depart. If so, you would see hope, joy, faith, and soberness in our eyes as we thank you for listening to our stories. You would hear us thank the Lord for his faithfulness in our lives and pray for his continued work in your life.

I imagine you are wondering where your road will lead. For some, it may lead to a harvest field among a people that have never heard the Good News of the death, burial, and resurrection of Jesus. For others, it may mean training the next generation of pastors to reach their own people. Some of your journeys may last decades, while others may be shortened unexpectedly. It is our prayer that all of you will experience the joy of seeing someone

CONCLUSION

become a child of God and transfer from the kingdom of darkness to the kingdom of light.

The commission you are considering or already surrendered to obey is worth it because Jesus is worthy of all honor, glory, and praise (Rev. 5:12). Your participation in God's mission is simply your humble, obedient response to God's revelation of himself, his will, and his ways. It is worship! We desire that the nations would know, enjoy, worship, and fear the one living God. May the Lord bless you for the sake of the nations!

PSALM 67

May God be gracious to us and bless us;
may he make his face shine upon us
so that your way may be known on earth,
your salvation among all nations.

Let the peoples praise you, God;
let all the peoples praise you.
Let the nations rejoice and shout for joy,
for you judge the peoples with fairness
and lead the nations on earth.
Let the peoples praise you, God,
let all the peoples praise you.

The earth has produced its harvest;
God, our God, blesses us.
God will bless us,
and all the ends of the earth will fear him.

Contributors' Biographies

Matt Bennett and his wife, Emily, grew up in Wisconsin, met and got married in Minnesota, and went to seminary in North Carolina. In 2011, they moved overseas and led a church-planting team sent out by their church until 2017. While in North Africa, Matt developed an interest in the academic study of Islam, which led him to pursue a PhD, where he explored the concept of the atonement as it appears in the Qur'an and the book of Hebrews. Since the fall of 2017, Matt and Emily have lived in Cedarville, Ohio, where Matt teaches as an associate professor of missions and theology and Emily oversees an English as a second language (ESL) program for immigrants and refugees. He is the author of *40 Questions about Islam, The Qur'an and the Christian,* and *Hope for American Evangelicals.*

Ryan Robertson has served as the president of Reaching & Teaching since April 2020. In 2018, Ryan left Canada and moved to Louisville, Kentucky, to take a role with Reaching & Teaching, a missions organization that assists local churches as they seek to make *mature* disciples, establish *healthy* churches, and train *local* leaders around the world. Ryan believes that the local church is both the means and the end of biblical missions. Ryan and his wife, Erin, have three children and are members of Third Avenue Baptist Church, where he serves as an elder. He is currently enrolled in the Doctor of Missiology program at The Southern Baptist Theological Seminary.

Jeff Kelly and his wife, Jamie, served for more than eleven years in the Middle East with their three sons, Isaac, Aaron, and Noah. While overseas, Jeff served as an elder, a team leader, and an associate cluster leader, working to reach Muslims in a densely populated urban context. Jeff has completed an MDiv in international church planting, an MA in intercultural studies, and an MA in economics in international development. In 2021, he completed the pastoral internship at Capitol Hill Baptist Church. Jeff loves the local church and loves seeing God's glory made manifest through local congregations around the world. Jeff now has the joy of pastoring in South Florida at First Baptist Church of Boynton Beach.

D. Scott Hildreth, along with his wife, Lesley, and two children, served in Europe and Central Asia for three terms with the International Mission Board. Their primary work was with Muslim people. Alongside his frontline responsibilities, they also helped with new missionary development. For the past fifteen years, Scott has led missionary sending and training at Southeastern Seminary, where he currently serves as associate professor of missiology and associate dean of ministry preparation. Scott has published several books and articles, including *Together on God's Mission: How Southern Baptists Cooperate to Fulfill the Great Commission*, *Sharing Jesus Without Freaking Out: Evangelism the Way You Were Born to do It*, and *Bondage and Freedom: Escaping the*

Trap of Pornography. He lives with Lesley in Raleigh, North Carolina. They have two adult children and three grandchildren.

Joshua Bowman served with his wife, Amy, and their four children in Zambia for eight years as rural church-planters among the Bemba people. He also served in South Asia as a church-strengthening strategist and team leader for nine years. He earned his MDiv from The Southern Baptist Theological Seminary and his PhD in missiology from Southeastern Baptist Theological Seminary. Josh is in his fifth year as assistant professor of theology and missions at Cedarville University. He is the author of *Cross-Cultural Missional Partnership* and a contributor to *The Quest of World Religions.* Josh's passion is to see healthy churches led by theologically sound leaders reach those who have never heard the gospel. He came to Cedarville from the mission field to mobilize, mentor, and encourage the next generation to participate in God's mission.

Joe M. Allen III served as an evangelist, church planter, and pastor trainer in South Asia among Muslims and Hindus from 2007 to 2021. He now serves as assistant professor of missions at Midwestern Baptist Theological Seminary, raising up the next generation of missionaries. He earned his PhD in applied theology from Southeastern Baptist Theological Seminary and his ThM from Dallas Theological Seminary. He also holds a BFA in graphic design from the University of Georgia. Joe is the author of a series of theology books for kids called Big Thoughts for Little Thinkers, which includes *The Trinity, The Gospel, The Scripture,* and *The Mission.* He is married to Christy, and they have two children, Claire and Joe IV.

BEFORE YOU GO

Matt Rhodes grew up in Southern California, finished high school in Scotland, and returned to the United States for college. He finished school with a master's degree in public health and worked as an epidemiologist before changing careers and moving overseas to serve as part of a church-planting team. Matt, his wife Kim, and their two sons are based in North Africa, where he has worked for the past twelve years among a previously unreached people group. Matt has recently begun translating the Bible with the help of others. He is the author of *No Shortcut to Success: A Manifesto for Modern Missions*.

Brian Harrell was born and raised on the mission field in Cape Town, South Africa. He earned a bachelor's and master's degree from Liberty University and an MDiv from Columbia International University. He returned to Africa with his wife, Becky, in 2004 to serve as church-planting catalysts among an unengaged, unreached people group (UUPG) in Northern Mozambique with the International Mission Board. He earned a PhD from Southwestern Baptist Theological Seminary while on the field. Brian and Becky have had the joy of raising four kids on the field. Sailing the Indian Ocean and hiking into remote villages to share the gospel, watching their boys learn to play "futebol" in the village, and their kids teaching English by flashlight are some of their favorite family memories. As a family, they have been blessed to know God's grace and faithfulness in fruitful ministry. Currently, Brian and Becky have the privilege of serving as cluster leaders for a great family of missionaries in the Central African Cluster.

CONTRIBUTORS' BIOGRAPHIES

Brooks Buser is a graduate of San Diego Christian College. After graduation, Brooks worked in finance and later as the CFO for a Dutch multinational. Eventually, he and his wife, Nina, felt the call to missions through the Scriptures and the confirmation of their church elders. In 2003, they left for the country of Papua New Guinea and spent thirteen years church-planting among the Yembiyembi people. By God's grace, they were able to develop an alphabet, teach the Yembiyembi how to read and write in their own language for the first time, teach Genesis through Revelation, translate the Scriptures, disciple elders and deacons, and see a strong church established among the Yembiyembi. In 2016, they returned to San Diego, and the following year Brooks was named president of Radius International. He now leads their four campuses around the world that train missionary candidates how to church-plant among the last unreached language groups on earth. Brooks holds an honorary PhD for his work in linguistics and Bible translation from his alma mater.

Zane Pratt serves as vice president for training with the International Mission Board of the Southern Baptist Convention. He also serves as an associate professor of Christian mission at The Southern Baptist Theological Seminary. He and his family lived and worked overseas, primarily in Central Asia, for twenty-three years before stepping into his current role. He is the husband of Catherine, the father of two grown children (both of whom were born and raised overseas), and the grandfather of two grandchildren.

Notes

1. I find Bobby Jamieson's thoughts on this idea of calling as it relates to pastoral aspirations helpful. Jamieson encourages the use of the biblical language of aspiring (1 Tim. 3:1) to describe an internal desire that is recognized as a calling when it is corporately affirmed by appointment (Bobby Jamieson, *The Path to Being a Pastor* [Wheaton, IL: Crossway, 2021], 20). The distinction between individual intention and corporate affirmation is equally helpful in the process of distinguishing those who personally aspire to be vocational missionaries and those who are called to the role by the affirmation of the congregation.

2. John G. Paton, *The Autobiography of the Pioneer Missionary to the New Hebrides* (Edinburgh: Banner of Truth, 2013), 25–26.

3. I'm grateful for Matt Burtch's early input and profound example of faithfulness in culture and language engagement.

4. John Calvin, *The Institutes of the Christian Religion* (Louisville, KY: Westminster John Knox Press, 1960), 3.2.24.

5. Richard Gaffin Jr., *By Faith, Not by Sight: Paul and the Order of Salvation* (Phillipsburg, NJ: P&R, 2013), 41–42.

6. Eugene Petersen, *A Long Obedience in the Same Direction* (Downers Grove, IL: IVP, 2000).

7. John G. Paton, *Missionary to the New Hebrides: An Autobiography* (Edinburgh: Banner of Truth, 1965), 200.

8. William Arndt et al., *A Greek-English Lexicon of the New Testament and Other Early Christian Literature* (Chicago: University of Chicago Press, 2000), 148.

9. Gordon D. Fee, *The First and Second Letters to the Thessalonians* in *The New International Commentary on the New Testament* (Grand Rapids, MI: Wm. B. Eerdmans Publishing Co., 2009), 326.

10. Dietrich Bonhoeffer, *Temptation*, trans. Kathleen Downham (London: SCM Press, 1955), 33.

11. J. D. Greear, "Sexual Sin, Broken Trust, and Disappointment," sermon delivered at The Summit Church, Durham, NC, February 26, 2023.

12. Paul David Tripp, "Trading One Dramatic Resolution for 10,000 Little Ones," Desiring God (website), December 29, 2013, accessed May 3, 2023, https://www.desiringgod.org/articles/trading-one-dramatic-resolution-for-10000-little-ones.

13. For more information about accountability and battling with pornography, see D. Scott Hildreth, *Bondage and Freedom: Escaping the Trap of Pornography* (self-pub., Kindle Direct Publishing, 2018).

14. Malcolm Gladwell, *Outliers: The Story of Success* (New York: Little, Brown and Company, 2008), 38–41.

15. Timothy Beougher, *Invitation to Evangelism: Sharing the Gospel with Compassion and Conviction* (Grand Rapids, MI: Kregel, 2021), 29.

16. Eckhard J. Schnabel, *Paul the Missionary: Realities, Strategies and Methods* (Downers Grove, IL: Inter-Varsity Press, 2008), 401.

17. J. I. Packer, *Evangelism and the Sovereignty of God* (Downers Grove, IL: IVP Books, 1961/2008), 78.

NOTES

18. Brian Zunigha, "Awkward Conversations Change Lives," Campus Ministry Today (website), October 2, 2016, accessed September 28, 2023, https://campusministry.org/article/awkward-conversations-change-lives.

19. More detail on this topic is available from Joe M. Allen III, "Getting Started with Gospel Conversations," Midwestern Baptist Theological Seminary (website), https://www.mbts.edu/2021/10/getting-started-with-gospel-conversations/.

20. Lemuel Haynes, "Divine Decrees: An Encouragement to the Use of Means" in *Black Preacher to White America: The Collected Writings of Lemuel Haynes, 1774–1833*, ed. Richard Newman (Brooklyn: Carlson Publishing, 1990), 99–100.

21. Joseph Alleine, "O Lord, Draw People to Christ!" in *Piercing Heaven: Prayers of the Puritans*, ed. Robert Elmer (Bellingham, WA: Lexham Press, 2019), 184.

22. John Piper, *27 Servants of Sovereign Joy: Faithful, Flawed, and Fruitful* (Wheaton, IL: Crossway, 2018), 520.

23. For further information about Radius International, please visit www.radiusinternational.org.